# READING
# Triumphs

Mc Graw Hill **Macmillan McGraw-Hill**

**RFB&D**
learning through listening

Students with print disabilities may be eligible to obtain an accessible, audio version of the pupil edition of this textbook. Please call Recording for the Blind & Dyslexic at 1-800-221-4792 for complete information.

B

The *McGraw-Hill* Companies

**Macmillan
McGraw-Hill**

Published by Macmillan/McGraw-Hill, of McGraw-Hill Education, a division of
The McGraw-Hill Companies, Inc., Two Penn Plaza, New York, New York 10121.

Printed in the United States of America

ISBN 0-02-192018-4
10 11 12 13 14  071  13 12 11 10 09

# C O N T E N T S

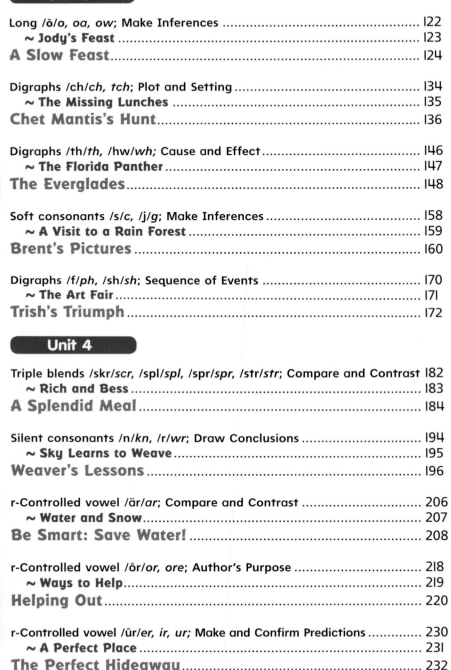

# Skills and Strategies

## Decoding

Read the words.

| | | | |
|---|---|---|---|
| miss | will | has | his |
| rip | at | mad | sick |
| dad | back | pick | ask |

## Vocabulary

| | | |
|---|---|---|
| tip | feel | ran into |
| jam | quit | acting |

## Comprehension

**Character and Plot** Characters are people in the story. The plot tells the events. A Story Map helps you analyze story structure.

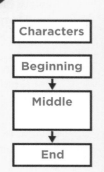

Characters

Beginning
↓
Middle
↓
End

Who are the characters?

## Pals for Ann

"Dad, I am mad," Ann said. "Tim and I ran into Sam. Sam asked Tim to bat with him. I was mad and ran."

Dad said, "You are in a jam. And you feel bad. I have a tip for you. Quit acting mad. Ask if you can bat with Sam and Tim."

Ann ran back to Tim and Sam. "Can I bat?" Ann asked. Now Ann, Tim, and Sam are pals.

Fill in a Story Map for "Pals for Ann." Retell the story.

# A Big Jam

by Chandra Brooke
illustrated by Heather Maione

Jack is in a jam. His pals are mad.

Tim is mad at Dan. Dan is mad at Tim.

Is Jack picking a pal? If Jack picks
Tim, Dan will get mad. If Jack picks
Dan, Tim will get mad.

## Dad Has a Tip

Jack tells Dad about his jam. "Tim will not be a pal if Dan is. Dan will not be a pal if Tim is."

Dad has a tip. "Tell Tim and Dan
how you feel. Tell them you will not
pick one pal."

## Picking Pals

Jack ran into Tim. Tim asked Jack
if he picked a pal.

"If I pick you, I will miss Dan. If I pick Dan, I will miss you. It is not fun."

Tim feels bad. "Okay, I will quit acting mad."

Jack and Tim see Dan. "Can we be pals?" Tim asks. "I am not mad."

"Okay, pal!" says Dan.

Jack has his pals back!

# Comprehension Check

## Retell

Read "A Big Jam" again. Fill in the Story Map. What happens at the beginning, middle, and end? Retell the story.

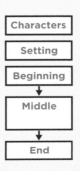

## Think About It

1. How did Dad help Jack?

2. Why is it hard for Jack to pick a pal?

3. Tell about one of your pals.

## Write About It

Tell about some problems pals have.
Tell how they fix their problems.

# Skills and Strategies

## Decoding

Read the words.

| | | | |
|---|---|---|---|
| best | mom | desk | sun |
| dog | pack | hug | did |
| long | hill | kept | pal |

## Vocabulary

| | | |
|---|---|---|
| letters | visit | treks |
| plans | explorer | |

## Comprehension

**Analyze Character** Every story has characters, setting, and plot. The main character is who the story is about. Use a Character Web to help you find a character's traits.

Character Trait

Clue    Clue

Find a character trait about Ned.

## Ned's Pen Pal

In class, Miss Bend tells Ned, "Send letters to a pen pal. Tell what you like to do."

Ned picks Ross. Ned tells Ross he treks on hills. Ned tells Ross he likes ponds with ducks and frogs.

Ross sends a letter back. He likes to swim and bike. Ross plans to visit Ned!

Ned tells Miss Bend, "Ross will be an explorer in a new land!"

Fill in a Character Web for "Ned's Pen Pal." Retell the story.

# Pen Pals

by Paula Taylor
illustrated by Julie Ecklund

## Tess Sends Letters

Tess has a pen pal. Tess sends Liz long letters. Liz sends letters back to Tess. Tess puts them in boxes.

Liz sends Tess letters about her
dog Bud. Bud pulls Liz in a dog sled.
Tess does not have a dog. She has a
black cat.

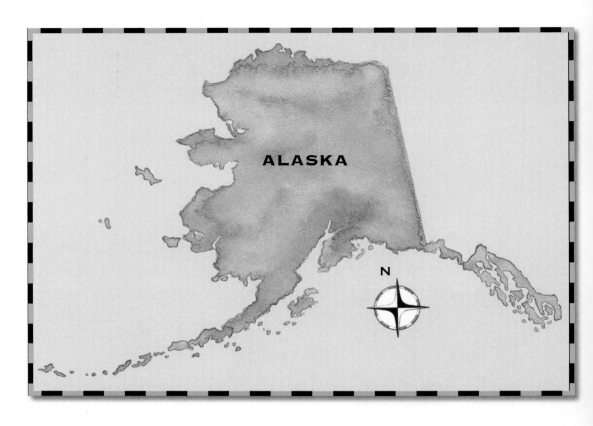

Liz asks Tess to visit. She says they can camp in a big tent with Bud.

Tess lets Dad see Liz's letter. Liz has sent a map. Dad says, "It is a long trek. But I can help you visit Tess."

At long last, Tess and Liz meet! Tess asks if Liz has plans. Liz says, "Yes! I am planning lots of trips."

## A Visit

Liz and Tess went on treks
with Liz's mom. The treks went
up big hills.

Liz's mom helped campers.
Liz had tips for them, too.

Tess had fun acting as an explorer.

As the sun set, Tess asked, "Must we get back?"

Tess had to pack up. Liz got sad. Tess hugged Liz and Liz felt better.

Liz and Tess were best pals as well as pen pals!

# Comprehension Check

## Retell

Read "Pen Pals" again. Retell the story.

## Think About It

1. What can you tell about Tess or Liz? Use the Character Web to help you.

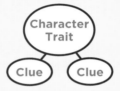

2. Why does Tess want to visit Liz?

3. What would you tell a pen pal about yourself?

## Write About It

If Liz had lived in a city, how would her plans have been different?

# Skills and Strategies

## Decoding

Read the words.

| | | | |
|---|---|---|---|
| twig | stop | leg | smell |
| track | stick | mud | slim |
| nest | snack | club | job |

## Vocabulary

| | |
|---|---|
| pests | objects |
| smart | slim |

## Comprehension

**Main Idea and Details**

The main idea is the biggest idea in a story. Details tell about the main idea. A Main Idea Chart can help you retell the selection.

| Main Idea | Details |
|---|---|
| | |
| | |
| | |

Find the main idea and details.

# Ant Jobs

An ant is an insect. It can be red, black, or brown. It can also be a pest at a picnic.

All ants do a job. An ant can lift a big object. An ant can drag a slim twig. You can see ants trek in a line on the sand. Maybe they are making an ant hill. An ant is smart as it does its job.

Fill in a **Main Idea Chart** for "Ant Jobs." Retell the selection.

# Ant Tricks

## by Greg Monroe

## Ants, Ants, Ants

An ant can be black, red, yellow, or brown. It has six slim legs. Some ants can have wings.

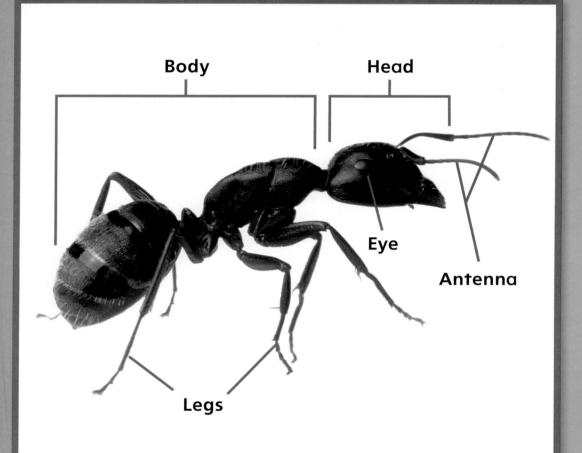

Body

Head

Eye

Antenna

Legs

An ant can lift big objects. Its six legs can help it lift and carry things. Six legs help it run fast. An ant's legs tap and tap as it runs.

## Jobs

An ant must have a job. One job is digging. Ants dig and help set up a nest. Other ants get twigs, mud, and sticks. They help fix up a nest.

Look at a sand hill. A big ants' nest is in it. Lots of ants can fit in a big nest.

Another ant job is to get food back to the nest.

## Pests

Ants can be big pests. Ants can get in boxes and bags of food. They can get in food left for pets. Ants can get on snacks and mess up a picnic.

Ants follow a smell to get more food.

When an ant finds a snack, it lifts a bit of the snack. It goes back to its nest. Can it find its way back to the snack? Yes! It has left a smell in its tracks.

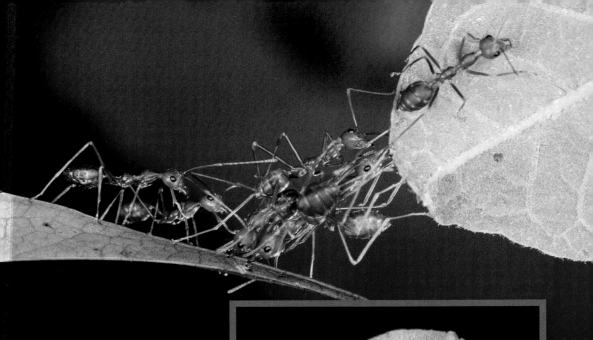

Ants work together to make a bridge.

An ant lifts a big leaf.

An ant is not big, but it is smart!

# Comprehension Check

## Retell

Read "Ant Tricks" again.
Fill in the Main Idea
Chart. Then use it to
retell the selection.

| Main Idea | Details |
|-----------|---------|
|           |         |
|           |         |
|           |         |

## Think About It

1. What things can ants do?

2. In what ways do ants work together?

3. Do you like ants? Why?

## Write About It

What do you know about other insects? How are they the same as ants?

# Skills and Strategies

## Decoding

Read the words.

| | | | |
|---|---|---|---|
| cape | swim | lake | glad |
| safe | take | same | plane |
| stuck | snake | made | frog |

## Vocabulary

| | |
|---|---|
| wetlands | lungs |
| tide | bills |

## Comprehension

**Main Idea and Details**

The main idea is the biggest idea in a story. Details support the main idea. A Main Idea Chart can help you retell the selection.

| Main Idea | Details |
|---|---|
| | |
| | |
| | |

Find the main idea and details.

# In The Wetlands

Wetlands are places close to water. Not all wetlands are the same. Wetlands can be near lakes or rivers or on a cape.

You can find bugs, ducks, and frogs in a wetland. You may see a frog take in air to fill its lungs. You may see a duck resting its bill in its wings. When the tide goes out, you may see a clam.

Fill in the **Main Idea Chart** for "In the Wetlands." Retell the selection.

# Wetlands

**by Lesley Noy**

## A Cape

A cape is a bit of land. It sticks
out in a lake or sea. It is a place to
rest in the sun. It can be fun to swim
at a cape.

Many kinds of grasses grow in a wetland.

A lot of land on a cape is wet.
The land is made of mud and sand.
Its name is "the wetlands."

# Wetland Frogs and Snakes

The best spot for a frog is a wetland. It jumps in a pond to keep its skin wet. But it must get out to fill its lungs.

Frogs and snakes make their homes in wetlands.

A water snake can be seen in wetlands. It can swim in a pond. And it can swim on top of the water. It hunts frogs and fish.

# Wetland Ducks, Clams, and Crabs

A black duck makes its nest in wetlands. It lays its eggs in its nest.

Ducks take naps. They tuck their bills in their wings and rest.

An American black duck swims in a pond.

Clams can grow to be twenty years old.

Wetlands have lots of clams. Clams dig in mudflats to be safe.

A mudflat is flat land. You can see a mudflat when it is low tide.

Tall grass can make clams safe from crabs and gulls.

Male fiddler crabs have one big claw and one small claw.

Crabs help grass get big. Crabs' claws dig in mud and sand. Digging brings food up to the grass.

It is best to take care of wetlands.
Wetlands help keep animals safe.

Cranes at a wetland.

# Comprehension Check

## Retell

Read "Wetlands" again. Fill in the Main Idea Chart. Retell the selection.

| Main Idea | Details |
|---|---|
|  |  |
|  |  |
|  |  |

## Think About It

1. What lives in a wetland?

2. How do the wetlands help animals?

3. How is a wetland different from where you live?

## Write About It

Why do we need to keep the wetlands safe?

# Skills and Strategies

## Decoding

Read the words.

| | | | |
|---|---|---|---|
| size | like | gave | smile |
| same | inside | fine | bite |
| five | name | hide | came |

## Vocabulary

| | |
|---|---|
| decide | hissed |
| gazed | trap |

## Comprehension

**Problem and Solution** A problem is what the character wants to do or change. The solution is how the problem is fixed.

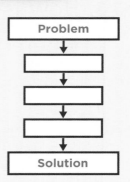

**Read**

What is the problem and solution?

# Mike's Cat

Mike gazed at the pets. He said, "If we got a cat, she could hiss at mice. We would not need mouse traps," begged Mike.

Mom said no. Mike had a plan. The pet store let kids spend time with the pets. He fed and petted a little black cat he liked.

Mom was surprised. She decided to let Mike get the cat after all.

Fill in the **Problem and Solution Chart** for "Mike's Cat." Retell the story.

# Jake's Pets

### by Abby Sims
### illustrated by Susan Hartung

Jake has dogs named Ike and Big Bess. Bess's name fits her size.

Jake also has two cats. Gus is tan. Mack is white.

## Jake Likes Us Best!

"Jake likes cats. Dogs are just okay," Gus said. Mack rolled on his back and gave a big smile.

"I bet Jake likes dogs best. Let him decide," said Ike.

Just then, Jake came in to get the dogs. "Ike! Big Bess!" Jake yelled. "Let's toss a ball."

Ike got his red ball. Bess ran and Ike jumped.

Mack and Gus gazed at Jake, Ike, and Big Bess.

Gus was sad. "Jake likes dogs best," said Gus.

"Jake will like cats. I have a plan," hissed Mack.

# Mack's Plan

Gus and Mack led the dogs to a crack in the wall. Mice liked to hide in it.

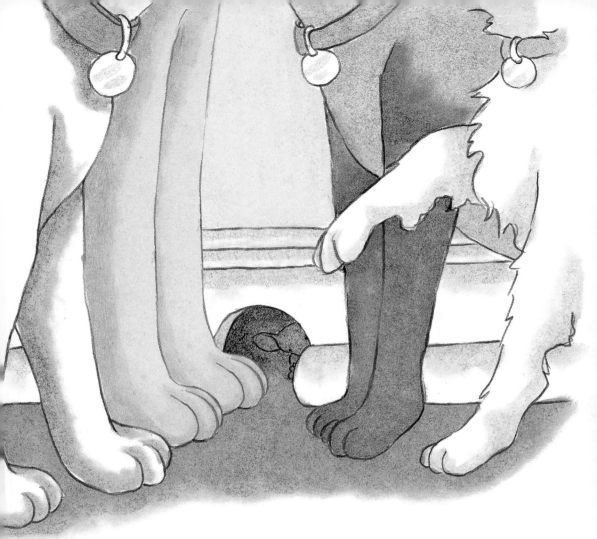

Mack and Gus hissed. Mack
stuck his paw inside. Five fast
mice ran past.

Jake used a trap and got the mice.

"Fine job," Jake patted Gus
and Mack.

Ike and Big Bess felt bad. "Jake likes cats more than dogs," said Big Bess. Ike and Big Bess got up to go out back.

Mack said, "Cats and dogs help Jake have fun. Jake likes cats and dogs the same." Ike and Big Bess smiled.

Later, Jake sat with his pets.

He said, "Pets are the best."

# Comprehension Check

## Retell

Read "Jake's Pets" again.
Fill in the Problem and
Solution Chart. Tell about
Gus and Mack's problem.
Retell the story.

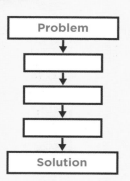

## Think About It

1. Why was Gus sad?

2. Why did the cats want to be
   Jake's favorite?

3. How do you take care of a pet?

## Write About It

Write about a time when you had
a problem. How did you fix it?

# Skills and Strategies

## Decoding

Read the words.

| | | | |
|---|---|---|---|
| flute | role | smile | cute |
| broke | tube | rule | home |
| like | joke | tune | close |

## Vocabulary

| | | |
|---|---|---|
| roles | practice | set |
| crowd | skilled | close |

## Comprehension

**Summarize** A summary tells the important parts of a story. A Story Map can help you summarize a story.

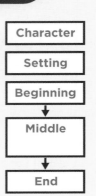

Find the beginning, middle, and end.

# A Cute Play

In my school play, I was a dog. My pal had the role of a cat. Our set looked like a yard. We made tree trunks out of tubes.

When the curtain opened, we saw the crowd. My pal and I said our lines. We had practiced a lot. Now we were skilled at acting!

Then I saw the curtains close. The crowd clapped. It was fun!

Fill in the **Story Map** for "A Cute Play." Summarize.

# Miss Pope's Class Puts On A Play

**by Anna Cragg**
**illustrated by Priscilla Burris**

## Cast

| Luke | Miss Pope | Rose |
|------|-----------|------|
| Cole | Mr. Duke | June |

# Planning A Play

**MISS POPE:** Our class play will be soon. Did you pick a story? Can we make a play from it?

**LUKE:** Yes, we can. June and I decided to pick tales about animals! We are using the tales to make a play.

**ROSE:** I like your plan, Luke! Let's make a play.

**JUNE:** Luke and I will make up the play. I will make lots of roles. It will have jokes and singing.

**LUKE:** Cole is a funny joker. He can tell jokes. And Rose can sing.

**COLE:** I can make a set. I can use mats, rugs, boxes, and desks. I can also open and close the stage curtains.

**ROSE:** June is skilled at crafts. She can make costumes. I will be her helper.

**JUNE:** We will ask Miss Pope if we can practice our roles in class.

# Practice

*Luke is just ending his acting practice.*

**LUKE:** At the end, I will gaze at a big wave.

**ROSE:** Nice acting job, Luke. Meg and Hope were very scared.

**LUKE:** Thanks, Rose. My role is fun. Did Cole make the set yet?

**JUNE:** Yes. The set is cute.

**ROSE:** June made cute costumes, too.

**JUNE:** Thanks, Rose. Let's go home and rest up.

# On Stage

*It is the next day. Mr. Duke is on stage.*

**MR. DUKE:** Miss Pope's class will act out a tale. Let's clap for Miss Pope's class.

Miss Pope's class sings songs and acts. Cole tells jokes. The crowd claps and waves as Cole tells his last joke. Miss Pope's class stands on stage and smiles.

**LUKE:** It is a hit! Rose is a good jazz singer. And Cole is a great joke teller!

**JUNE:** Miss Pope said we can take pride in our play.

**ROSE:** I like acting and singing. Next time I will pick a tale to tell!

# Comprehension Check

## Summarize

Read "Miss Pope's Class Puts on a Play" again. Fill in the Story Map. Summarize.

## Think About It

1. Why is June chosen to make the costumes?

2. Why do kids practice the play?

3. Would you enjoy planning a play? What would you do?

## Write About It

What makes someone a good planner of a play? Explain.

# Skills and Strategies

## Decoding

Read the words.

| | | | |
|---|---|---|---|
| leave | seem | team | green |
| tune | creek | home | speed |
| please | froze | speak | lead |

## Vocabulary

| | | |
|---|---|---|
| sunset | gleamed | usually |
| deeds | trust | |

## Comprehension

**Fantasy and Reality** Fantasy is what happens in a story that could not happen in real life. Fill in the Fantasy and Reality Chart to help you find what is fantasy and what is reality.

| Fantasy | Reality |
|---|---|
| | |
| | |
| | |

What is fantasy? What is real?

## A Bedtime Story

Sunset was Willie Wolf's bedtime. The sunlight gleamed through the trees. Willie's mom usually told him a story.

"Once there was a little cub that did good deeds. All the animals trusted him. As a gift, the Queen Wolf gave him dreams. Now the little cub can dream as he sleeps."

Willie drifted off to sleep.

Fill in the **Fantasy and Reality Chart** for "A Bedtime Story." Summarize.

# Mom Wolf Speaks

by Todd Lilly

illustrated by
Marianne M. Sachs-Iacob

## Swimming and Running

Mom called her pups. "Rex! Cubby! Huck! Come on. It is time to leave."

Cubby sat close to the grass.
"Can I please practice swimming?"
he begged.

He was a good swimmer.
His wet coat still gleamed.

"No," said Mom. "It is time
to leave."

"Let's race!" yelled Huck.

"I bet I will win," cried Rex. Rex and Huck ran at top speed. They were skilled at running.

The cubs spotted three kids. Manny, Eva, and Rosa seemed lost and scared.

The big green forest was home to deer, rabbits, foxes, and snakes.

Men came and chopped trees. Men hunted. Mom did not trust men but she did like kids. Mom had seen these kids in the past.

## A Snake!

A soft hiss came from the grass.

Eva, Manny, and Rosa froze in their tracks. Manny spotted a snake! Eva screamed.

Mom wolf had to help. "Keep still," snapped Mom.

Mom stepped out from the trees. Huck helped the snake creep back in the grass. Mom asked the kids, "Are you lost?"

"Yes," wept Rosa.

"You can speak?" asked Manny.

"Yes," said Mom.

"We usually just speak to each other. We howl. But we also speak up if kids need help," said Mom.

Mom added, "We help kids because we see your fine deeds. We've seen Eva feed deer. We have seen Manny set a trapped rabbit free."

Manny, Eva, and Rosa sat and petted the cute pups.

Mom said, "You need to get home before sunset. The creek will lead home."

Manny and Eva got up and
waved to Mom and her pups. Rosa
patted Rex. The pups howled and
romped home.

# Comprehension Check

## Summarize

Read "Mom Wolf Speaks" again.
Summarize.

## Think About It

1. Why is the story
   not real? Fill in the
   Fantasy and Reality
   Chart.

   | Fantasy | Reality |
   |---------|---------|
   |         |         |
   |         |         |
   |         |         |

2. Why does Mom Wolf not trust men?

3. How is Mom Wolf like someone
   you know?

## Write About It

How are the wolves in the story like
people? How are they like animals?

# Skills and Strategies

## Decoding

Read the words.

| | | | |
|---|---|---|---|
| flying | happy | night | sky |
| dry | find | clean | kind |
| high | light | queen | flight |

## Vocabulary

| | | |
|---|---|---|
| sights | hobbies | plastic |
| early | blades | different |

## Comprehension

**Fact and Opinion** A fact is something that can be proven. An opinion is a belief that might

| Fact | Opinion |
|------|---------|
|      |         |
|      |         |
|      |         |

not be supported by facts. Use the Fact and Opinion Chart to help you find facts and opinions.

Find facts. Find opinions.

# Gliders and Planes

A hang glider is a beautiful sight. It has fabric pulled over a metal or plastic frame. When a glider flies in the sky, it is bright and colorful. It is best to glide early at sunrise.

Prop planes are different from gliders. The spinning blades help it take off. A plane is better because it flies higher than a glider. Flying and gliding are fun hobbies.

Fill in the **Fact and Opinion Chart** for "Gliders and Planes." Summarize.

# Flight
## Gliders to Jets

by Lee Cho
illustrated by Dick Smolinski

People expect to have fun flying. The best sights can be seen from high in the sky.

Flying is fun. But some kinds of flying can be more fun than other kinds.

## Gliders

Gliders came before planes.
Gliders use wind to fly.

Wings on an early glider flapped
up and down. To get a glider up,
men ran on the sides. When winds
lifted the glider, the men let go.

Hang gliding over a beach.

Hang gliding is one of the best hobbies. A hang glider is different from early gliders. It is a frame with a big kite set on top. Hang gliders ride on wind like a kite.

Unless it is foggy, a glider is the best way to see from up high.

A glider plane carries only one or two people.

A glider plane is a light plane. It has long, slim wings, but it has no engine.

A glider plane is usually pulled up in the sky by an airplane. After the glider lifts up, the plane lets go. The best thing about a glider plane is how quiet it is.

A twin engine propeller plane has an engine on each wing.

## Planes and Jets

The first plane with an engine was a prop plane. A prop plane has spinning blades. As the blades spin faster, the plane lifts up.

December 1955: A *Comet 3* passenger jet flies in the sky.

The first jet plane flight was in 1939. A jet is bigger and flies faster than a prop plane.

A jet can fly across the U.S. in about six hours.

The best thing about a jet is its speed. A jet can fly at 885 miles an hour. It is four times as fast as a race car.

Like a car, a jet uses lights at night. The lights gleam in the sky.

The inside of this jet has two levels.

Jets can be big. One of the biggest has up to 555 seats. Its wing span is almost as wide as a football field.

July 14, 2001: The first test flight of the solar-electric Helios flew for 18 hours.

## What is Planned Next?

Planes will be made of plastic. Plastic makes a plane lighter. It will use less gas.

Next, planes might not use gas. A plane might run on just sunlight! That is the best flight plan yet!

# Comprehension Check

## Summarize

Read "Flight: Gliders to Jets" again. Fill in the Fact and Opinion Chart. Summarize.

| Fact | Opinion |
|------|---------|
|      |         |
|      |         |
|      |         |
|      |         |

## Think About It

1. What will planes be like in the future?

2. Why is a glider plane quiet?

3. Would you fly in a glider? Why?

## Write About It

How do fast planes help people?

# Skills and Strategies

## Decoding

Read the words.

| | | | |
|---|---|---|---|
| stand | trunk | blend | bright |
| cling | night | drink | swift |
| bring | spend | light | fly |

## Vocabulary

| | | |
|---|---|---|
| danger | clump | cling |
| swift | scales | |

## Comprehension

**Summarize** The main idea is the most important point in a story. Details explain the main idea. A Main Idea Chart helps you find important information.

| Main Idea | Details |
|---|---|
| | |
| | |
| | |

Find the main idea and details.

# Staying Safe

Animals have many ways to stay safe. Some animals hide or run away. Some can warn others with their bodies.

Skunks make a stinky smell when they are in danger. A rabbit can hide in a clump of grass. A bat might cling to a branch up high. A swift squirrel runs up a tree trunk if it is chased. A snake with green scales can hide in the grass. All animals try to stay safe.

Fill in the **Main Idea Chart** for "Staying Safe." Summarize.

# Animal Hide and Seek

**by Jill Viera**

**illustrated by Karen Bell**

## Hiding In Grass

Can you see a green grasshopper hiding here? Its legs seem like grass stems. It can cling to a blade of grass and keep out of sight.

The grasshopper is hiding from a mouse! The mouse is up early. It will spend time hunting bugs. But it will not spot the grasshopper.

The grasshopper uses its green color to hide in a clump of grass. It can't hide on a tree trunk. It won't blend in.

## Seeking A Meal At Night

A bat can't see colors. But it can see well at night. It can see the bright cactus flowers in the moon's light. It drinks from the flower and flies away.

A moth eats at night as well.
But owls can eat moths! If an
owl gets close, a moth will fly off
its flower. If the moth is swift, or
fast, it will get away.

## Keeping Eggs Safe

Can you spot a nest? It seems like
a pile of rocks and grass. But it is a
nest of spotted eggs! Quails can keep
their eggs safe in a nest like this.

## Warning Colors

A snake can have bright colors on its scales. Bright colors can act as a warning. They might mean, "Get back! My bite will make you sick!"

If a deer can tell danger is close,
it can warn others to run! It can't
speak, but it has a neat trick.

It will stand still and lift its tail like
a flag. The sudden bright white tells
other deer to run and hide.

## Hide and Seek

Using colors to hide keeps animals safe. Using colors to seek helps animals get food to eat. Hide and seek can help animals live!

# Comprehension Check

## Summarize

Read "Animal Hide and Seek" again. Fill in the Main Idea and Details Chart. Summarize.

| Main Idea | Details |
|---|---|
|  |  |
|  |  |
|  |  |

## Think About It

1. How do animals use color?

2. How do quails keep their eggs safe?

3. Tell one thing about an animal that surprised you.

## Write About It

What are some ways people warn each other of danger?

# Skills and Strategies

## Phonics

Read the words.

| | | | |
|---|---|---|---|
| tray | mailbox | faint | claim |
| draft | rain | print | stay |
| brain | stain | mail | gray |

## Vocabulary

| | | |
|---|---|---|
| draft | flames | routes |
| habits | invented | |

## Comprehension

**Author's Purpose** An author writes to entertain, inform, or persuade. An Author's Purpose Chart helps you decide why the author wrote the selection.

| Clues |
|---|
| |
| |
| |

↓

| Author's Purpose |
|---|
| |

Find the author's purpose.

## Ben Franklin Fights Fire

Long ago, some cities didn't have fire squads. A draft could make many homes catch fire. If homes caught fire, people helped put out the flames. Ben Franklin set up a fire squad. He made a map with routes to find the homes. Ben explained that safe habits would help stop fires.He even invented a stove that heated homes!

Fill in the **Author's Purpose Chart** for "Ben Franklin Fights Fire." Summarize.

# Ben Franklin

by Carrie Dillon

illustrated by Susan Avishai

Ben Franklin was a smart man. He spent time reading. Reading helped him think of many handy objects he could make.

## A Stove

In Ben's day, a fireplace let in a draft and let heat out. Ben invented a stove that kept heat inside his home. It used less wood as well.

Years later somebody made his stove better. Even though that man fixed it, he didn't rename it. It is still "the Franklin Stove."

## A Lamp

In Ben's time, street lamps were lit by flames at night. Smoke from flames made a gray stain on the glass. The light was dim and faint.

Ben made lamps with bright light. His lamps let out smoke. Ben's lamps didn't get gray inside.

# Swim Fins

Do you use swim fins? Ben Franklin invented them!

Ben Franklin liked to swim and play in water. He made fins for his hands. His fins did not work well.

Then he remade swim fins for his feet. He could kick more water at a time and swim just like a fish!

## Lightning Rods

In June 1752, Ben had a plan. He got a kite and put a wire on it. He tied on a key. Then he went out in the rain.

Ben's kite went up high. He waited for lightning. Lightning went from the wire to the key. It stopped at the key.

In Ben's day, lightning was a danger to homes. It set them on fire. Ben made a lightning rod.

The rod acted like his key and dragged lightning away from the homes. Lightning rods still keep homes safe today.

# Mail

Ben liked to get mail. Mail was not swift in his day. It wasn't easy to get mail to mailboxes.

Ben claimed that running mail night and day would make it faster.

He set up routes to help mailmen find homes and mailboxes. Mail trucks still use these routes today.

## Printing

Ben had a job as a printer. He printed and reprinted pages using a printing press like this.

Ben had to take big, heavy trays to the press. He liked to say he could lift two trays at a time.

Ben got up early. He didn't stay up late often. He felt that his habits helped him to feel good.

Maybe his habits helped him to be smart, as well!

# Comprehension Check

## Summarize

Read "Ben Franklin" again. Summarize. Tell the most important ideas.

## Think About It

1. Find clues. What is the author's purpose?

2. How did Ben Franklin make homes better?

3. What did Ben Franklin invent that you like the most? Why?

| Clues |
|---|
|  |
|  |

↓

| Author's Purpose |
|---|

## Write About It

Why do you think people like Ben Franklin so much?

# Skills and Strategies

## Decoding

Read the words.

| | | | |
|---|---|---|---|
| loaf | road | bowl | roast |
| slow | told | toast | replay |
| explain | oatmeal | waiter | yellow |

## Vocabulary

| | |
|---|---|
| midday | large |
| feast | complete |

## Comprehension

**Make Inferences** Use story clues and what you know to make inferences. Use an Inference Map to list the clues.

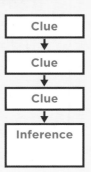

Find clues to make inferences.

# Jody's Feast

Jody went to Mr. Tony's fruit stand. Mr. Tony had a load of plums he couldn't sell. He gave them to Jody.

Jody told her pals to come by at midday. They made pies, jam, and large turnovers!

"This feast is not complete without Mr. Tony," Jody said. She invited him over and showed him the pies. He was glad he gave Jody the plums.

Fill in the **Inference Chart** for "Jody's Feast." Summarize.

# A Slow Feast

## by Tim Brady
## illustrated by Robert Neubacker

Miss Sloan did not like the midday meal at school. Kids ate fast and they did not eat well. So Miss Sloan made a plan.

"We will make a big feast," explained Miss Sloan. "Bring in something you eat at home. It must not be fast. It must be slow."

## Not Fast, Just Slow!

"What do you mean by slow?" asked Bo.

"It is something that takes time to make and eat. Make it at home. Bring your homemade meals to class on Monday. We will set up a midday feast!"

The bell rang and the kids ran into the sunlight.

Bo spoke up, "I like snacks that I can eat fast."

"Miss Sloan explained that we need better eating habits. She said we must not eat fast food all the time," replied Joan.

## Eggplant

Joan told Mom and Dad about the feast. Joan's dad smiled. "Will your pals like oatmeal?"

"No," Joan replied. "I need a meal for lunch!"

"We can make eggplant," said Mom. "Dad can grill it."

## Dumplings

"Whoa!" yelled Jill's dad. "What's going on here?"

"Jill must take a slow food to class," Mom replied.

"Mom told me we can make steamed dumplings," said Jill.

Dad hugged Jill. "If your mom is making it, your pals will like it!"

## Sea Bass

Rick watched Mom making a sea bass. "We roasted it with yellow peppers. Now it must cook slowly on a low flame."

Dad came running in. "I have greens for a salad."

"Thanks, Dad. A loaf of bread will complete the meal!" Rick said.

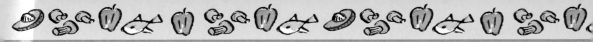

## A Big Pot of Rice

"What can I take?" Bo asked.

"We can make rice with green beans, carrots, and toasted nuts," said Bo's dad. "Grandma used to make this kind of rice."

"Oh yes!" Bo cried. "I can't wait! I will take a big pot of rice!"

## The Feast

On Monday, kids in class held bowls and plates.

"I made eggplant," said Joan.

"Dad and I made rice!" added Bo. "I cut up green beans and added toasted nuts."

The kids ate a large meal. They tried roasted eggplant, stuffed grape leaves, meatloaf, refried beans, and egg rolls.

Miss Sloan smiled. There were no high fat sweet treats.

"I like slow food!" exclaimed Bo.

# Comprehension Check

## Summarize

Reread "A Slow Feast." Fill in the Inference Chart. Summarize.

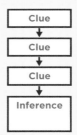

## Think About It

1. Why didn't Miss Sloan like the midday meal?

2. How do you think this feast helped the kids eat better?

3. How can you learn about healthy foods?

## Write About It

Why is healthy food good for your body?

# Skills and Strategies

## Decoding

Read the words.

| coat | branch | check | soap |
| cheek | reached | coast | peach |
| catch | lunchtime | stitch | patch |

## Vocabulary

coast is clear    office    unlatched

clutched    boasted

## Comprehension

**Analyze Story Structure**

The plot is what happens in a story. The setting is where and when it takes place. A Setting Web helps you find clues that tell about the setting.

Identify the setting.

## The Missing Lunches

Mitch sat on a chair in the principal's office. He was on a case. Someone stole the teachers' lunch bags at the school.

He waited until the coast was clear. He unlatched the lock on the teachers' lunch room. He saw the robbers munching happily and clutching carrots. It was bunnies that stole the lunches! Mitch boasted that he had solved another case.

Fill in the **Setting Web** for "The Missing Lunches." Summarize.

# Chet Mantis's Hunt

**by Don Branch**
**illustrated by Marc Mongeau**

## Missing Drops!

It was lunchtime. Chet Mantis tapped his belly. "Where can I eat lunch? Maybe *Mister Bug's* or *Wet Grasses*..."

Peach Buzz ran in to his office. "Chet, I need help," snapped Peach.

Peach was mayor of Bug Box. It was unlike Peach to ask for help.

"The Hanging Drops are missing. Someone unlocked the case and stole them." said Peach. The Hanging Drops had hung in Buggy Hall for a long time.

"We will find the drops," said Chet. He was glad to be on a case.

Chet had a plan. He knew Batty Bat was back in town. Batty played mean tricks on bugs. Peach had sent him away last winter. Now he was free. It was just like Batty to steal the drops.

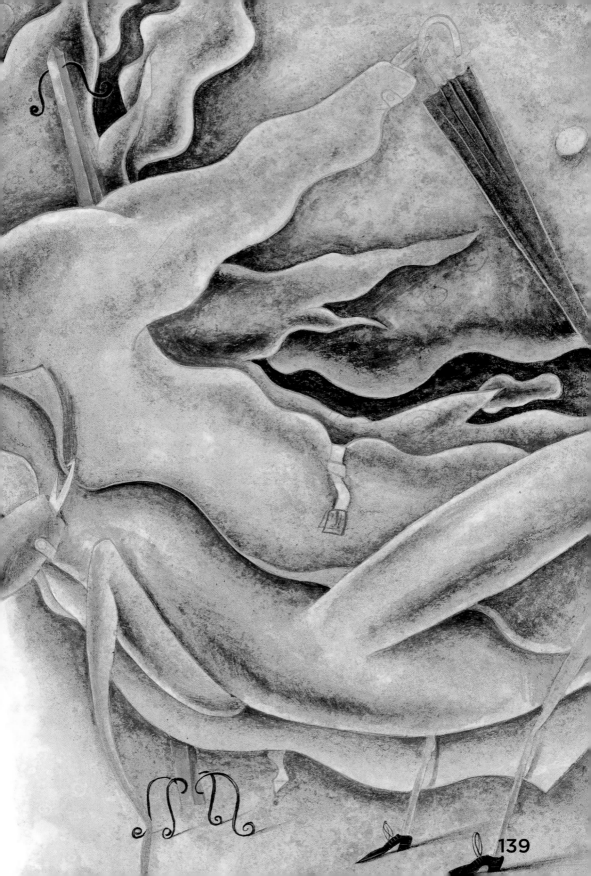

## The Hunt Is On

Chet blended in with a leaf and watched Batty's gang.

"Did you see the drops?" asked Mugsy.

"Yes!" replied Dizzy. "But Batty hid them until the coast is clear. Then we will sell the drops for a lot of cash."

Chet tapped his cheek. "If I were a robber, where might I hide stuff?"

Chet had seen Batty watching bugs. Batty watched from a high branch of a large oak tree. The oak was next to Buggy Hall. It seemed like a fine spot to check.

Chet was right! The drops hung
just behind the tree. He reached up
and unlatched them. Chet slipped the
drops in his coat.

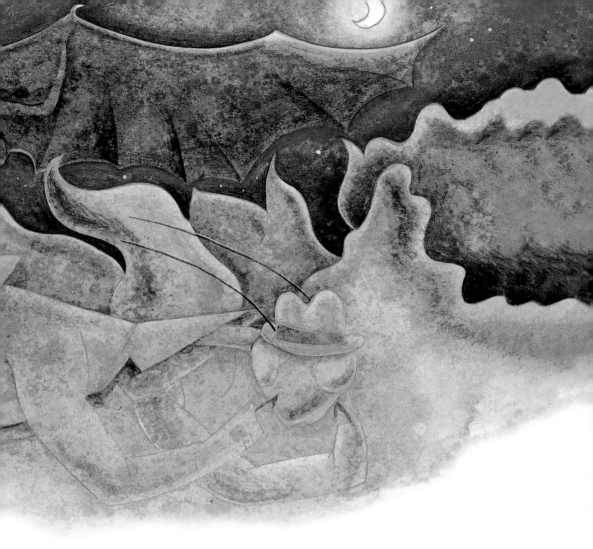

Chet spied Batty flying over the road. He crept to a patch of green grass and blended in.

Batty soared right past! Chet clutched the drops in his coat and ran fast!

Chet got to a safe spot and reached in his coat. He held up the drops. They sparkled like raindrops. Batty had lost! "Peach will be so pleased," he boasted.

He got home late and was quite hungry.

"Well," thought Chet. "Maybe I will feast at Happy Seeds."

# Comprehension Check

## Summarize

Reread "Chet Mantis's Hunt."
Fill in the Setting Web.
Summarize.

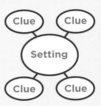

## Think About It

1. How does the setting help Chet find out about the missing drops?

2. Why does Batty Bat steal the hanging drops?

3. Write about a time when you had to find something that was lost.

## Write About It

Why was Chet happy to help Peach?

# Skills and Strategies

## Decoding

Read the words.

| | | | |
|---|---|---|---|
| thump | which | catch | panther |
| each | teeth | thick | these |
| white | think | wheel | chill |

## Vocabulary

| | | |
|---|---|---|
| wildlife | pounds | beneath |
| drained | river | protect |

## Comprehension

**Cause and Effect** A cause is why something happened. The effect is what happened. Use a Cause and Effect Chart to find causes and effects.

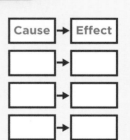

Find the cause and effect.

# The Florida Panther

Some wildlife in the Everglades is in danger. The Florida Panther is a big cat. It can be 150 pounds! When it walks, the leaves crunch beneath its feet. Only 30 to 50 panthers roam the land.

Long ago people drained the rivers to make land for houses. Many animals left. Panthers had little to eat. Today people work to protect these panthers and where they live.

Fill in the **Cause and Effect Chart** for "The Florida Panther." Summarize.

# The Everglades

by Carrie Dillon
illustrated by Robert Casilla

Take a trip with us in the
Everglades. This land is wet. It is a
swamp. Some call it a river of grass.
It is home to many animals.

We must use a boat to get to each spot. My dad can push this boat with a long pole. The land is not deep beneath the water.

Let us see if we can find wildlife.

## Wildlife

This is a panther. It has long whiskers. It is a cat as big and fast as a tiger. It can get as heavy as a grown-up man!

These big cats rest in daytime. They hunt deer and rabbits at night. Unlike many big cats, panthers can swim well.

This is a wood stork. When it gets hungry, it sticks its beak in the water. Then it opens its beak and waits. When a fish swims by, the beak snaps shut! The stork catches the fish in its beak.

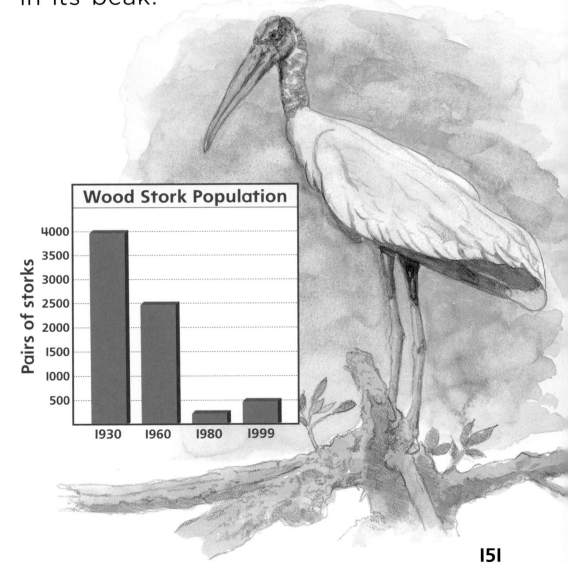

**Wood Stork Population**

Pairs of storks

| 1930 | 1960 | 1980 | 1999 |

## Big Animals

We can find an alligator in the Everglades as well. An alligator can blend in with the grass. It may seem slow when its tail drags on land. But when it is time to run, it lifts up its tail. Then it can run fast!

An alligator has at least 70
teeth! If the teeth fall out, they
just grow back.

Here is a manatee. It has thick, gray skin. It can be as heavy as a cow. A manatee can munch 100 pounds of sea grass each day. That is like eating the grass off a whole baseball field.

## Keeping Animal Homes Safe

There was a time when people drained the water to use the land. The animals and plants needed water. When the land dried, the animals left.

Then rules were made to protect the land. Water was put back and made clean. People stopped making homes on this land. Then the plants and animals returned.

Now it is a fine land to visit. Take a ride with us anytime.

# Comprehension Check

## Summarize

Reread "The Everglades." Summarize.

## Think About It

1. Why did animals leave the Everglades? Use the Cause and Effect Chart.

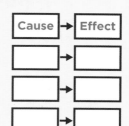

2. Why are manatees called "sea cows"?

3. Which of the animals did you like best? Why?

## Write About It

Why must we keep the Everglades clean?

# Skills and Strategies

## Decoding

Read the words.

| | | | |
|---|---|---|---|
| huge | edge | gym | city |
| danger | age | nice | beneath |
| think | change | decide | bridge |

## Vocabulary

| | | |
|---|---|---|
| imagined | ancient | tilted |
| ledge | mist | amazing |

## Comprehension

**Make Inferences** You
need to use story clues
and what you already

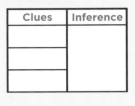

| Clues | Inference |
|---|---|
| | |
| | |

know to make inferences. Use the
Inference Chart to make inferences.

What inferences can you make?

## A Visit to a Rain Forest

Grace stepped up to the ledge. She tilted her head back to see the ancient stones. Ages ago people placed them there. A mist hung in the forest. It was amazing.

Grace listened to the wildlife. It was louder than she imagined. Birds seemed to shout. Grace was happy to visit a rain forest.

Fill in the **Inference Chart** for "A Visit to a Rain Forest." Summarize.

# Brent's Pictures

by Rod Harrington
illustrated by Will Sweeney

This is a picture of us as we packed
for our camping trip. I had packed my
gym bag. Mom helped Chuck. He had
packed just his stuffed animals!

# Going on a Trip

This is Dad. He is planning which roads we will take. Dad said it may take five days. He added that it will be nice to leave the city.

He made long green lines to show which roads we might take.

We filled the space in back of the van. We had to take tents, bags, snacks, and camping stuff.

We crossed ten states. It seemed to take ages. Chuck and I played games to pass the time. Chuck said he missed home. Then he went to sleep.

## Camping

The trees were much higher than
I imagined! Lots of these ancient trees
are at least 2,000 years old! Maybe
a kid stood in front of this tree back
then. At that time this tree trunk was
just a stick.

It was odd standing beneath the giant trees. I tilted my head back to see the tops. Chuck and I felt like ants standing next to the huge tree trunks.

We woke up to see a big bear
on a picnic table. It was bigger than
I imagined. Campers had left a package
of treats. The bear ate the treats.

We watched it from inside the van.
Chuck was frightened. When the bear
left, we packed up to leave.

On the way home, I had to take a picture of this. We camped so high up that the clouds sunk beneath us. I crossed a bridge and stood on a ledge. It was the highest I had ever been. I felt a mist in the air. It was amazing!

I told Mom and Dad that I had a blast on this trip! I told them that I might take a long camping trip when I am older. I will hike up bigger hills. I will camp up higher!

Mom and Dad smiled. I think they liked my plans.

# Comprehension Check

## Summarize

Reread "Brent's Pictures."
Fill in the Inference Chart.
Summarize.

| Clues | Inference |
|---|---|
|  |  |
|  |  |
|  |  |

## Think About It

1. How do you know that Brent likes taking pictures?

2. Why did they watch the bear from inside the van?

3. How would you plan a trip for you and your family?

## Write About It

Why do people visit parks?

# Skills and Strategies

## Decoding

Read the words.

| | | | |
|---|---|---|---|
| huge | fresh | shape | swish |
| photo | sheets | shine | phone |
| brush | ledge | finish | elephant |

## Vocabulary

sketches idea gathered

perfect triumph ramp

## Comprehension

**Sequence** The sequence is the time order of events in a story. Look for clue words like *first*, *next*, and *last*. A Sequence Chart helps you put events in order.

| Event |
|---|

What happens first, second, and last?

# The Art Fair

Joseph liked to paint. He made sketches first. Then he gathered his paint brushes and fresh paper. He worked until each painting was perfect. Mom said it would be a good idea to enter the art contest.

Joseph entered and won! What a triumph! Joseph was proud as he walked up the ramp into the school. The paintings were beautiful.

Fill in the **Sequence Chart** for "The Art Fair." Summarize.

# Trish's Triumph

**by Donna Diaz**

**illustrated by Lorraine Sylvestri**

Trish loved painting. She was careful with her brushes. She kept them nice and clean. She always placed the paint tubes back in the case when she finished painting.

# A Painting Contest

Trish's pals stopped by to visit. Trish missed school. She had stayed home since the accident. The school didn't have a wheelchair ramp.

"Trish, there is a painting contest next week," exclaimed Shannon. "And the winner gets a prize!"

"You must enter," added Phillip.
"Your paintings are beautiful. I bet
you will win."

"Thanks, Phillip," replied Trish.
Trish thought about the painting she
had made of her class last winter.

The next day, Trish sat for a long time. She watched her cat Ralph from a window. He sat on the ledge outside.

She tried to come up with an idea. She kept on thinking all day.

## Trish's Paintings

Trish's mom gathered books that might be useful. They both looked for pictures that could be helpful.

Trish placed brushes and sheets on her desk and waited. Then she had a big idea. Trish made sketches and showed them to her mom and dad.

Her mom and dad liked the sketches.

"I think this sketch can hang on the wall," stated Trish. "But there is a problem. I thought of a better idea for the contest. And it needs to be much bigger than this. I cannot find paper big enough to hold it."

Dad had a helpful plan. He went outside with Trish. He showed her where she could paint.

Trish sketched some shapes on a big wall. Then she used a brush and swished fresh paint on it. It was perfect!

Trish painted every day until she finished. It was the biggest painting she had ever made.

Trish's pals loved it. It was a colorful painting about summer. It showed kids diving in a swimming pool. Trish was in the pool playing. A huge cheerful sun shone on the water.

Trish won first place! It was amazing! A man came and took a photo. The photo was shown in the paper.

Trish used the prize money to get a ramp made at school. She was so thankful. Trish was going back to class! It was a joyful triumph.

# Comprehension Check

## Summarize

Reread "Trish's Triumph."
Fill in the Sequence Chart.
Summarize.

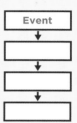

## Think About It

1. How did Trish get a wheelchair ramp to go to school?

2. Why did Trish paint a picture of herself swimming with friends?

3. How do you think her picture made people feel? Why?

### ✎ Write About It

Why was it important for Trish to return to school?

# Skills and Strategies

## Decoding

Read the words.

| | | | |
|---|---|---|---|
| stripes | three | spring | shave |
| scrape | shrug | throw | scream |
| splash | trophy | shrimp | thrill |

## Vocabulary

recipe   rise         flat as a pancake

batter   splendid

## Comprehension

**Compare and Contrast**

To compare is to find things that are alike. To contrast is to find differences. A Venn Diagram shows what is alike and what is different.

Different
Alike

Compare and contrast the characters.

# Rich and Bess

Rich and Bess are twins. Rich likes to bake. Bess likes to throw baseballs. Rich says, "Bess, I have a new recipe. Will you help?"

Bess says, "Yes, but my cakes don't rise. They are as flat as a pancake." But the new recipe is for pancakes. Bess scrapes the bowl and pours the batter. She flips the pancake and catches it!

"You did a splendid job!" says Rich.

Fill in the **Venn Diagram** for "Rich and Bess." Summarize.

# A Splendid Meal

by Lee Cho
illustrated by Dom and Keunhee Lee

## Mixing It

Kim and Lang planned to make dinner for their mom. Lang put on a navy blue apron. Kim put on one with green stripes.

Dad made a big fresh salad. Josh helped fill and roll up the spring rolls.

"This recipe says 'place 3 tsp of shrimp filling inside each roll.' What does 3 tsp mean?" asked Josh.

Kim replied, "It means three teaspoons. Each roll gets three teaspoons of filling."

Lang licked the mixing spoon. "Yuck!" she cried. "This batter tastes bad!"

"We have not put everything in yet," said Kim as she swept up.

"'Add one pt of milk.' How much is a pt?" asked Lang.

"A pint is two cups. Fill that cup up twice," said Kim.

Kim and Lang greased and floured
the baking pans. Kim was careful
with her pan but Lang was not.

Kim scraped the batter into each
pan. She waited for Dad.

Kim and Lang set the table as Dad put the cakes in the oven.

"I feel like something is missing," sighed Lang.

"Why? I think it will come out fine," shrugged Kim.

Just then Josh yelled from the kitchen. "Kim! Lang! I think we have a problem!"

## Fixing It

Each cake was flat as a pancake.

"Oh! I forgot the baking powder!" Kim cried.

"Does baking powder make cakes rise?" asked Josh. Kim nodded.

"We will have to throw it out," sighed Kim.

"Wait! I have an idea!" Lang ran to the freezer. Lang got a tub of ice cream.

"It can be an ice cream cake!" she exclaimed.

Lang spread ice cream between the cakes.

"We all scream for ice cream," Josh joked.

"Get ready to scream, 'Hi, Mom!'" said Kim. "I think she is here."

The family gathered at the table. Mom had a splendid meal. She ate spring rolls, salad, and three slices of cake!

Josh joked, "Kim and Lang invented a secret cake recipe."

Mom exclaimed, "That is the best cake I have ever tasted!"

# Comprehension Check

## Summarize

Reread "A Splendid Meal." Summarize.

## Think About It

1. How are Kim and Lang alike? How are they different?

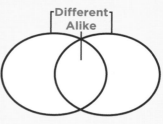

2. Do you think Kim or Lang is a better cook? Why?

3. Tell about a meal you would prepare for someone.

## Write About It

Why do people like to share meals?

# Skills and Strategies

## Decoding

Read the words.

| | | | |
|---|---|---|---|
| wrote | knots | knee | knuckles |
| writer | wrong | knock | string |
| wrists | strong | knit | stretch |

## Vocabulary

| | | |
|---|---|---|
| earn | wrap | passed |
| wring | beamed | get along |

## Comprehension

**Draw Conclusions** Find clues from the story and use what you know to draw conclusions. A Conclusion Map helps you make inferences and draw conclusions.

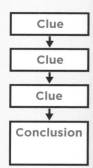

Draw conclusions about the story.

## Sky Learns to Weave

Sky wanted to know how to weave. The weaver said Sky had to earn the lessons. Sky put on a knitted wrap and went out. She passed through the village. She knocked on the weaver's door. The weaver told Sky to wring out the wash. Sky did as she was told.

The weaver beamed. Sky had strong wrists. Sky knew then that they would get along.

Fill in the **Conclusion Map** for "Sky Learns to Weave." Summarize.

# Weaver's Lessons

by J.D. Gable
illustrated by Arvis Stewart

Weaver knows how to make warm
blankets and rugs. Each day, she sits to
weave. Her knuckles move quickly as
she ties little knots. Her wrists bend as
she weaves at her loom.

# Woman With No Name

One day Weaver heard a knock. A stick was tapping on a ladder.

A woman called, "I am lost and cold. I am on the wrong path. I do not know how to find my way."

Weaver replied, "Use a ladder and step inside."

The woman went down the ladder.
"I went to gather wood. I got lost."

"Tell me your name," said Weaver.

"I am called Woman With No Name.
I lost my name when I did not get
along with others."

198

"You must earn your name back," replied Weaver.

"Teach me to weave and knit. My people can wrap themselves in blankets. Then I will get my name," begged the woman.

"Kneel beside me and unwrap this yarn. We will begin lessons," replied Weaver.

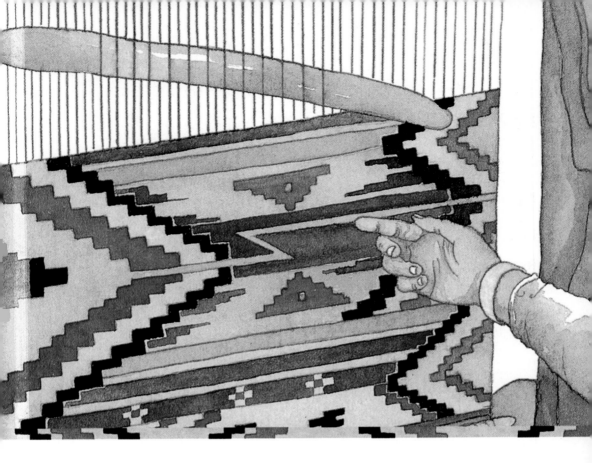

# The Weaving Lesson

Weaver showed Woman With No Name how to weave. "Think kind thoughts as you weave. They will be woven in the blanket. But make a path so they can get back to you."

Woman With No Name made a path in the rug just as Weaver had showed her. "That is well made," nodded Weaver.

A week passed. "It is time to go back home," Weaver explained. "Teach your people how to weave. Make wraps to keep warm."

Woman With No Name beamed a smile. She felt thankful. "I will teach them well," she replied. She carried her bundle into the cold.

## Working Together

Woman With No Name went home. She gave tasks to her people. She asked them to rise early to get the tasks done.

She melted snow to wash wool and wring it dry. Women sheared the sheep. Children helped stretch the wool to dry. Men made a strong loom.

Then Woman With No Name showed the children the way to spin wool. She showed them how to weave and knit. She was a gentle teacher.

The people made splendid rugs and blankets.

After a while, the Woman With No Name earned back her name: Shell Woman.

Shell Woman spent her life teaching people weaving. She never forgot the kindness of the Weaver.

# Comprehension Check

## Summarize

Reread "Weaver's Lessons."
Fill in the Conclusion Map.
Summarize.

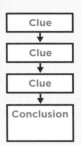

## Think About It

1. How did Woman With No Name earn her name back?

2. How did she help her people?

3. Tell about a time when you helped someone.

## Write About It

Name ways people help their neighbors.

# Skills and Strategies

## Phonics

Read the words.

| | | | |
|---|---|---|---|
| part | shark | start | wrinkle |
| hard | know | smart | yard |
| marsh | harmful | knot | written |

## Vocabulary

| | | |
|---|---|---|
| liquids | streams | tap |
| remember | dusk | supply |

## Comprehension

**Compare and Contrast**

To compare is to find things that are alike. To contrast is to find differences. A Venn Diagram shows what is alike and what is different.

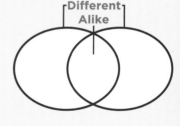

Compare and contrast liquid and solid water.

# Water and Snow

Water can be a liquid, like rain or water in a stream. Water can also be a solid, like ice or snow.

Tap water can be used for drinking and washing. But remember to turn it off so you don't waste water.

Snow falls in the winter. It can be pretty falling in a park at dusk. But it's hard and sharp when it's icy.

Water is useful as liquid and solid.

Fill in the **Venn Diagram** for "Water and Snow." Summarize.

# Be Smart: Save Water!

## Fresh Water and Salt Water

Did you know that three-fourths of Earth is covered by water? Most of this water is salt water.

Humans drink and use fresh water. But most of the fresh water is frozen. We mustn't waste what we have.

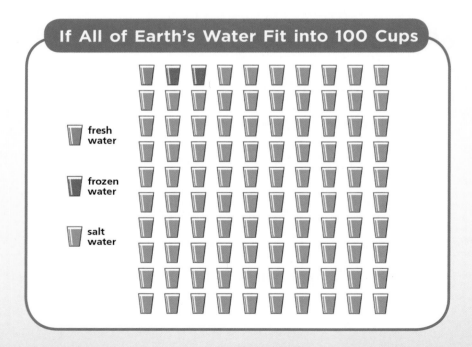

If All of Earth's Water Fit into 100 Cups

fresh water

frozen water

salt water

## Who Needs Water?

It's well known that people, animals, and plants need water to live. All must get along to share the planet's fresh water supply. All use water to drink.

# People

People need to drink water. More than half of a person's body weight is water. Our bodies need to replace up to three quarts of water each day. We get some water in the foods we eat. But we also need to drink liquids each day.

Drinking water helps food move through our bodies. It also helps keep our bodies at the right temperature.

Your body is about 70 percent water.

We use water for other things. We use it when we wash our bodies and brush our teeth. We use it when we wash and cook food. We use it to wash clothes.

We play in water. On hot summer days, we might splash in a lake. In the cold winter, some of us play in the snow. Snow is frozen water!

Swimming is a great way to stay cool in the heat.

Dolphins can live in fresh or salt water because they breathe air.

## Water Animals

Water animals cannot live outside the water. Their skin must stay wet.

Water animals live in both salt and fresh water. Oceans are salt water. Rivers, streams, and most lakes are fresh water. Marshes can be salt or fresh water.

Whales, dolphins, sharks, and fish live in the oceans. Fish, frogs, and snakes live in fresh water.

# Land Animals

Land animals use water in the same way that people do. They drink water and use it to cool off their bodies.

Animals in the desert get water from plants. A desert pack rat drinks liquid from a cactus plant.

# Plants Need Water

A plant can't get food from the ground without water. Water flows up the stem to the leaves. The sun beams down and helps the plant make food. Water helps bring food to other parts of the plant.

Farms need water for their crops to grow.

## How Much Water Do You Use?

| ACTIVITY | WATER USE |
|---|---|
| Running the tap | 3 to 5 gallons a minute |
| Brushing Teeth | 2 to 5 gallons |
| Flushing Toilet | 1.5 to 4 gallons each flush |
| Washing machine | 35 to 50 gallons |
| Washing the car | 50 gallons |
| Taking a bath | 40 to 50 gallons |
| Taking a shower | 5 to 10 gallons a minute |

# Be Smart: Save!

Saving water is smart. Wasting water is wrong. Here are some ways to start saving.

- Remember to shut off water when not in use.

- Fill a bottle of water instead of running the tap each time.

- Take less time in the shower.

- Water yards and plants at dusk.

Earth is sometimes called "The Water Planet."

Water covers most of the planet. But we can drink and use just a small part of it.

It is not hard to save water, so start saving. We can help the planet stay alive.

# Comprehension Check

## Summarize

Reread "Be Smart: Save Water!" Fill in the Venn Diagram. Summarize.

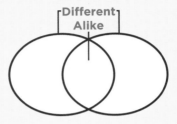

Different
Alike

## Think About It

1. How do animals use water in different ways than people?

2. Why is it important to save water?

3. How can you save water?

## Write About It

What would the world be like without water?

# Skills and Strategies

## Decoding

Read the words.

| | | | |
|---|---|---|---|
| score | start | porch | store |
| before | horse | parks | north |
| harm | morning | storm | short |

## Vocabulary

| | | |
|---|---|---|
| projects | talents | chore |
| collected | agree | ignored |

## Comprehension

**Author's Purpose** An author writes to entertain, inform, or persuade. An Author's Purpose Chart helps you decide why an author wrote a story.

| Clues |
|---|
| |
| |
| |

↓

| Author's Purpose |
|---|

Find the author's purpose.

# Ways to Help

There are many ways to help others. Think of projects that use your talents. It won't be a chore if you have fun!

Hold a bake sale with some pals. Take the money you've collected and agree to give it to a good cause. If you sing, hold a concert for sick kids.

Don't ignore people in need. You can always give a smile. Even smiling is a way to help!

Fill in the **Author's Purpose Chart** for "Ways to Help." Summarize.

# Helping Out

by Tanya Sturz
illustrated by Sally Springer

## Helping Is Fun

Helping feels good. It gives you a nice feeling inside. So reach out and help!

There are lots of ways to help. You can help people, animals, or the land. Helping out can be a chore. But it also makes you feel proud.

You can help by
holding a car wash
for your school.
You can help by
reading to children.
You can help by
making Get Well
cards for sick people.

# Start a Club

Why not start a club? You can do a lot by yourself, but you'd do more with a club. In a club, kids can combine their talents.

Every kid has a talent. One kid might be good at planning projects. Another kid might be good at building things.

In a club, each member gets time to share their ideas. Each kid needs to feel that he or she is helping. It's not fun if someone feels ignored. Everyone must get along.

Give your club a name. A name can tell the ways a club will try to help. A club that helps by cleaning up beaches might be named, "The Clean Shore Club."

Pick a name that will be simple to remember. Each member of the club should agree on the name.

## More Ways to Help

A toy drive is a nice way to get things for kids in need. Ask people to give new or slightly used bats, dolls, games, or other things.

**225**

After the toy drive, take the toys to hospitals or shelters. You'll be helping kids in need.

Think of fun ways to help. Rake leaves or sweep a porch for people you know. Pick up trash by a park or stream.

Hold a food drive. That's when canned food from the store is collected. Then the food goes to people who are hungry.

In time, a club might grow big. More
kids will wish to help. Ask them to
pitch in. Maybe they can be members
as well. It is nice to share the feeling
you get by helping!

# Comprehension Check

## Summarize

Reread "Helping Out." Summarize.

## Think About It

1. Find clues that tell the author's reason for writing this story.

| Clues |
|-------|
|       |
|       |
|       |

↓

| Author's Purpose |
|------------------|
|                  |

2. How can a club help people?

3. Why do you feel glad when you help someone?

## ✎ Write About It

Write a list of ways to help people.

# Skills and Strategies

## Decoding

Read the words.

| | | | |
|---|---|---|---|
| burn | girls | fort | dirty |
| perfect | before | germ | short |
| shirt | turn | bird | church |

## Vocabulary

| | |
|---|---|
| shady | bored |
| wonder | perked |

## Comprehension

**Make and Confirm Predictions** A Predictions Chart helps you check your understanding. Make predictions about what events might take place.

| What I Predict | What Happens |
|---|---|
| | |
| | |
| | |

Make and confirm predictions.

## A Perfect Place

Jada sat against a big shady tree. She liked being alone but she was bored. She petted her purring cat that was curled up next to her. She listened to the birds chatter. She wondered what there was to do.

Then she perked up. "I know. I will make a tree house!" She ran to get her girl friends. They worked together and made a tree house.

Fill in the **Predictions Chart** for "A Perfect Place." Summarize.

231

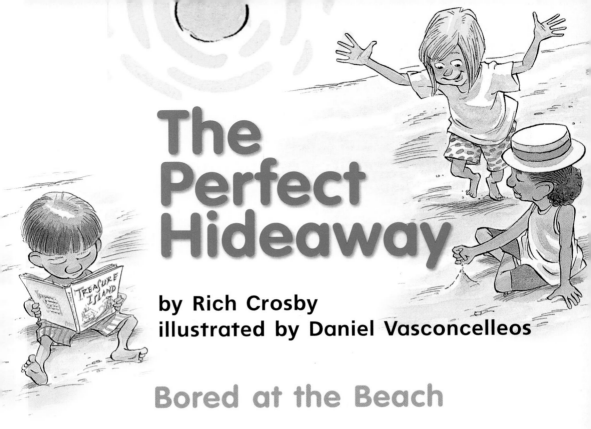

# The Perfect Hideaway

**by Rich Crosby**
**illustrated by Daniel Vasconcelleos**

## Bored at the Beach

Last summer, Miranda, Jack, and Kate stayed at the beach.

Miranda ran sand between her fingers. Jack read a book. The girls were bored.

"We need to stir things up!" Kate yelled. "Let's make something big."

"Like what?" Miranda asked.

Kate said, "Let's make a hideaway."

Jack got up. "Okay! We can set it up between those three trees over there," he said.

"It will be a huge chore. Let's find a shady place to sit." Miranda sighed.

"It will be fun," begged Kate. "You can get in first. It will be the shadiest spot on the beach."

"Fine," nodded Miranda, "But I still think it's too hot."

Jack went to find some planks. The girls started to collect tree branches. Suddenly, a boy ran by with a sheet on his head.

"Who is that kid?" asked Kate.

"I've never seen him before," replied Miranda.

"I wonder what he's doing," said Kate.

"I found three short planks. Those kids grabbed the best stuff," Jack told the girls.

"Which kids?" asked Kate?

"Didn't you see them? Those kids behind the bait house," said Jack.

"A kid ran by with a sheet. Maybe he is with them," replied Kate.

# A Better Plan

"I see them!" yelled Miranda.

Three kids were dragging a wagon with a big piece of driftwood in it.

"They are setting up a fort on the side of the bait house," added Jack.

Just as Miranda, Kate, and Jack got the hideaway set up, it began to rain.

"I'm dirty and tired," complained Jack.

"And I'm still bored and hot," sighed Miranda

Kate perked up. "It's nice in here. Why don't we go meet those kids when the rain stops?"

"Yes," nodded Miranda. "With six kids, we can play lots of games!"

At the bait house, a kid was holding his nose. "I bet it smells like fish over there," said Kate. "They don't look happy. Let's invite them over."

Jack strolled over to the kids. "Let's make one big hideaway."

"We were thinking the same thing! I am Kirby. Mark and Shirley are my friends," explained one of the kids.

"It's nice to meet you. Let's get going!" exclaimed Jack.

Shirley, Jack, and Miranda pulled the wagon, while the others pushed it.

"We will make a perfect place to rest!" exclaimed Kate.

"Yes. But it's getting hot," panted Miranda. "I can't wait to be in the shade!"

# Comprehension Check

## Summarize

Reread "The Perfect Hideaway." Use the Predictions Chart. Summarize.

| What I Predict | What Happens |
|---|---|
|  |  |
|  |  |
|  |  |

## Think About It

1. Did you think the kids were going to work together? Why?

2. Why didn't a hideaway help the kids be less bored?

3. Why do kids make hideaways?

## Write About It

Tell about a time when kids worked together to make something.

# Skills and Strategies

## Decoding

Read the words.

| | | | |
|---|---|---|---|
| crazy | cocoa | diner | stable |
| music | silent | solar | human |
| baby | final | tiny | frozen |

## Vocabulary

| | | |
|---|---|---|
| nearby | demanded | owned |
| special | customers | survive |

## Comprehension

**Sequence** Sequence is the time order of events in a story. Look for clue words like *first*, *next*, and *last*. A sequence chart helps you put events in order.

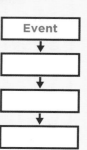

What happens first, next, and last?

# Pizza for Breakfast

Jacob owned a pizza parlor. Customers came for lunch and dinner. But they went to nearby places for breakfast. He didn't know if his parlor could survive. He needed a plan.

First Jacob made a special pizza with egg and hash browns. Next he made pizza with berries and yogurt. Last he made pizza pancakes! Soon people demanded his breakfast pizzas. It was a triumph!

Fill in the **Sequence Chart** for "Pizza for Breakfast." Summarize

243

# The Great Ice Cream Shop Turn Around

**by Jim Flaherty**
**illustrated by Deborah Melmon**

David Kramer ran the famous Kramer's Ice Cream Shop. He sold ice cream with all kinds of toppings. He had sprinkles, nuts, whipped cream, and even bits of fruit.

David worked hard in the summer. All day he would place perfect circles of ice cream on cones.

### The New Store

Kramer's Ice Cream Shop did well during the summer months. But as the weather turned colder, he sold less ice cream. He felt ignored.

This year he had a new worry. Recently, an ice cream store opened nearby. He wondered if he would lose his customers.

David stood by the sidewalk and looked at the new store. He could hear music from the shop. The balloons in front made it look cheerful.

David knew that his ice cream was the best. He had been making it for years.

At first David was sad. Then he got angry. Finally he thought, "That store's ice cream cannot taste better than mine. They must be doing something to make people go there. I need to find out why!"

# An Ice Cream Talk

David hurried over to the big store at closing time. He saw they had lower prices.

"May I help you?" asked a lady. "My name is Rachel."

"Why are your prices so low?" David demanded.

"I need lower prices to get customers." said Rachel.

He told her he owned the shop across the street. He said he was worried about her taking his customers.

David went home. He could lower his prices. But he did not know if his shop would survive.

"What will make people eat ice cream when it's cold out? How can I get people to come to my shop?" David asked himself.

Then he came up with a plan. He asked the lady from the big store to come over.

David explained his idea. "We need to make both stores special. I like to make new ice cream flavors like black currant ice cream. People like trying unusual flavors."

"That is perfect!" Rachel exclaimed. "I can make ice cream sandwiches and bake banana muffins. I can also make frozen fruit pops. We can sell hot apple cider as well!"

They worked hard. Both stores sold hot drinks during the winter, which was very helpful.

People loved the unusual ice cream flavors. The frozen fruit pops and muffins tasted great.

Soon the shops were working full time. Each store had a long line of customers. David's plan had worked!

# Comprehension Check

## Summarize

Reread "The Great Ice Cream Shop Turn Around." Fill in the Sequence Chart. Summarize.

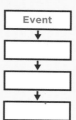

## Think About It

1. Why was David worried after the shop across the street opened?

2. Why did the shops need to work together?

3. Why do more people like ice cream in summer?

## Write About It

How else could the shops have worked together?

# Skills and Strategies

## Decoding

Read the words.

| | | | |
|---|---|---|---|
| robot | wood | paper | stood |
| book | brook | notebook | took |
| cookie | bagel | goodbye | barefoot |

## Vocabulary

| | | |
|---|---|---|
| united | laws | basic |
| childhood | important | |

## Comprehension

**Cause and Effect** A cause is why something happened. The effect is what happened. Use a Cause and Effect Chart.

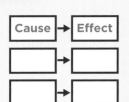

Find a cause and effect.

# Unions

The United States has many laws to protect workers. Some laws say that people must stop work to eat and sleep. These are basic needs. There are laws that say kids must not work long hours. Childhood is important.

If a company ignores these laws, people can make a union. The union and the company can work together to make things better.

Fill in the **Cause and Effect Chart** for "Unions." Summarize.

# Dolores Huerta: She Took a Stand

by Anna Cragg

illustrated by Robert Casilla

## A Look at the Children

Dolores Huerta looked at her class. Some children looked tired and hungry. They had no shoes. They came to class barefoot.

Dolores sighed. These were the children of farm hands. Dolores knew why childhood was hard for them.

Farm hands move often. They pick crops on nearby farms. When they finish, they move to the next crop. The children cannot stay in the same school.

Often the kids were behind in reading and math. They did not stay in school long enough to learn basic lessons.

In one school the kids might sit in a third grade class. At the next school, the same kids might be placed in first grade.

## Life as a Farmhand

In the 1950s farmhands were not treated well. Pickers made less than a dollar a day. Bosses at big farms did not help the families if workers got hurt. Farmhands often slept in their cars or trucks.

Dolores's mom ran an inn. Often she let farmhands stay free at her inn.

Dolores loved her work as a teacher. She could help children in her class. Books and teaching were important. But she wanted to help more farmhands and their kids.

## The United Farm Workers

In 1955, Dolores stood up for farm hands. She made speeches. She demanded that states make good laws to help the farm hands. She helped them fill in papers so they could vote.

Dolores met a man named César Chávez. He also tried to help farm hands. Dolores and César asked farmhands to join them in a union named the United Farm Workers.

Dolores and César tried to make big farms treat workers better. They believed that farms must pay fair wages and make work safe.

But big grape farms still did not treat farmhands well.

In 1965 the United Farm Workers decided to strike. A strike is when workers think something is unfair. They decide not to work until the problem is fixed.

Dolores helped stage a boycott on grapes. People did not buy grapes. Sales dropped. Big farms lost money.

In 1971 the big farms agreed to give farmhands things like clean drinking water. Farmhands also got a rest time during the workday.

Dolores kept fighting for those who needed help.

Dolores Huerta began with a wish to help kids in her class. In her lifetime she helped more than she could imagine.

# Comprehension Check

## Summarize

Reread "Dolores Huerta: She Took a Stand." Fill in the Cause and Effect Chart. Summarize.

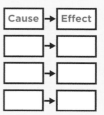

## Think About It

1. Why did Dolores stop teaching?

2. How did she help farmworkers?

3. What would you do if you saw someone being treated in an unfair way?

## Write About It

What problems happen when people don't have homes or money to live?

# Skills and Strategies

## Decoding

Read the words.

| | | | |
|---|---|---|---|
| balloon | drew | good | chew |
| soon | troop | news | book |
| stew | stood | flew | smooth |

## Vocabulary

| | | |
|---|---|---|
| interest | designs | crew |
| pilot | breathe | |

## Comprehension

**Fact and Opinion** A fact is something that is true. An opinion is based on a belief. Use the Fact and Opinion Chart.

| Fact | Opinion |
|---|---|
| | |
| | |
| | |
| | |

Look for facts and opinions.

# Floating in the Sky

Hot-air balloon designs are colorful. If you have an interest in balloons, you should go for a ride.

First, the crew gathers supplies. Then the pilot checks the wind. Soon the balloon floats up.

Some people are afraid that they can't breathe in a hot-air balloon. But they are wrong. It's easy and fun to fly in a balloon.

Fill in the **Fact and Opinion Chart** for "Floating in the Sky." Summarize.

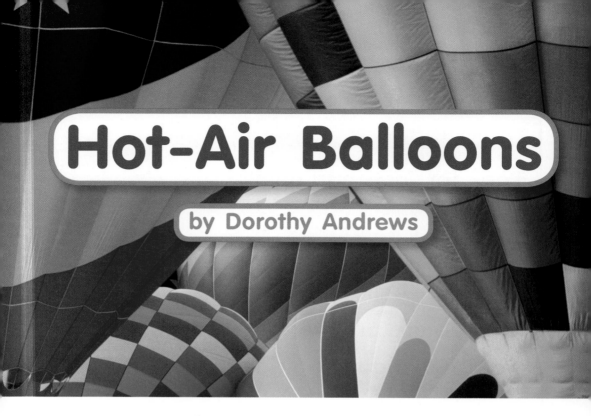

# Hot-Air Balloons

## by Dorothy Andrews

### The Roots of Flight

What was the best thing that ever happened for flight? It was making a paper bag float in air. It happened too long ago for TV news. But don't be fooled. It was important.

Here is what happened. Two French men stood in a kitchen. They held a paper bag over a fire. The bag filled with hot air and it lifted up. Why was this good news?

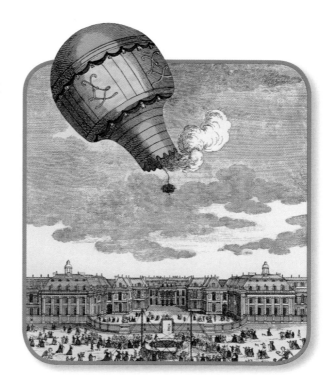

The first hot-air balloon flight took place in France.

The men felt the bag was proof people could fly. They made a huge balloon and filled it with hot air. The first test flight had no crew.

Some felt it might be unsafe for people to go up. The air might be too thin to breathe. So they sent a duck, a rooster, and a sheep in the next flight. The animals came back safely. After that, people went up. This happened in 1783.

## Uses of Hot-Air Balloons

Soon people used balloons for many things. They flew them for fun. They traveled from place to place in them.

Balloons were used in wars. They were used as tools for spying. From the balloons, riders could see enemy troops far away. The balloons also took supplies to the troops.

This balloon was used by the Navy in wartime.

Balloons are hard to steer. They rarely return to where they took off.

The first planes did not replace balloons. But in time, basic planes got bigger, better, and faster. Soon fewer and fewer hot-air balloons were in use. People believed balloons would soon be forgotten.

But that hasn't happened. People have a renewed interest in hot-air balloons. Balloons are back and are better than ever!

The pilot's crew mixes propane and fire. It makes very hot air.

Why can hot-air balloons fly? It's because they become lighter than air. To rise, the air inside a balloon must be lighter than the air outside. Hot air is lighter than cool air. It can lift a balloon up.

The pilot must know which way the wind is blowing.

It takes special skill to fly a hot-air balloon. Getting it in the sky is just part of the job. If it needs to go higher, the pilot adds more hot air. Less hot air brings it lower. If the pilot is skillful, it is smooth sailing.

Many beautiful balloons at a festival.

Why is hot-air ballooning still a good sport for today?

One reason is that it is exciting to ride in a balloon. Besides being fun, it doesn't pollute. It is quiet. And a balloon doesn't need a long runway.

Balloons can take odd shapes.

Hot-air balloons are blooms of color in the sky. Most people think today's balloons are pretty. The balloons have bright colors and fun designs. It is easy to like them.

On a balloon ride, you can see for many miles.

Things may take us farther and faster in years to come. But we flew hot-air balloons long before planes were invented. And we'll keep flying hot-air balloons for a long time yet.

# Comprehension Check

## Summarize

Reread "Hot-Air Balloons."
Use the Fact and Opinion
Chart. Summarize.

| Fact | Opinion |
|------|---------|
|      |         |
|      |         |
|      |         |

## Think About It

1. Find one fact. How do you know it is a fact?

2. Why do writers put opinions in stories?

3. Would you like to ride in a hot-air balloon? Why?

## Write About It

Name reasons why people fly hot-air balloons.

# Skills and Strategies

## Decoding

Read the words.

| | | | |
|---|---|---|---|
| noise | voice | blew | boy |
| loom | destroy | soil | join |
| voyage | moist | drew | choice |

## Vocabulary

| | | |
|---|---|---|
| guided | soil | village |
| listened | distant | expert |

## Comprehension

**Make and Confirm Predictions** If you predict what happens next, you can check how well you are reading. Use the Predictions Chart to check your predictions.

| What I Predict | What Happens |
|---|---|
| | |
| | |
| | |

Can you guess what will happen next?

## Royal Saves His Village

Jim's dog Royal loved to swim. One day, Royal would not go in the lake. He held up his moist paw and pointed to a distant spot. Royal guided Jim along the muddy soil. Jim saw that a can of poison had spilled in the lake.

Jim called the police. A water expert stopped the water flow. It was good Jim listened to Royal. Royal saved the village!

Fill in the **Predictions Chart** for "Royal Saves His Village." Summarize.

# The Sheep Herder

**by Lesley Noy**
**illustrated by Robert Casilla**

## A Boy Tends His Sheep

Oscar lived in a small village in Peru. He helped his mom and dad tend sheep after school.

Each day, Oscar took the sheep up on a hill to eat. He liked tending sheep but he dreamed of doing something great.

At night Oscar enjoyed resting on a big blanket. He listened to the distant noise of the bleating sheep. He heard the voices of his family in the stillness of the night.

He liked to lie awake thinking about books he had read. He enjoyed pretending that he was a boy in one of the books. In his mind, he took long voyages to far-off lands.

One night a huge rainstorm hit his little village. The river overflowed and flooded many buildings. The mud began to slide down the hillside. The mud slide was so heavy that it destroyed a wall of his school.

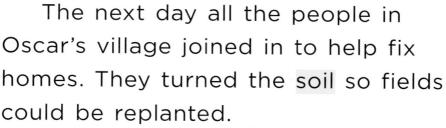

The next day all the people in Oscar's village joined in to help fix homes. They turned the soil so fields could be replanted.

Oscar helped the sheep avoid the moist soil. Sheep have little feet that sink in mud. Oscar guided the sheep to a place to graze.

## Oscar Brings Happiness

That night at dinner, Mom said, "The children in the village need to return to school. We must fix it. But there is no money to pay for supplies."

Dad told Oscar that the school books were destroyed by mud.

Oscar told Mom and Dad that he would help. He would think of a way to rebuild the school.

The next day Oscar watched the expert weavers in his village. Their fingers danced on the loom to make beautiful designs. Oscar knew people in distant lands would like these blankets.

He sent small woven samples to his cousin, Carlos, in the States. He asked Carlos to find people who might want to sell the blankets.

Then Oscar sketched a picture of his village. He thought people would like to see where the blankets were made.

He drew the mountains behind his herd of sheep. He enjoyed watching the sheep graze by the river.

He sent the picture to his cousin.

Carlos wrote back after three weeks. He found a shop that wished to sell the blankets. The shop would hang Oscar's picture behind the blankets.

Oscar proudly showed the letter to his dad. He wrote and thanked Carlos for his help and kindness.

Oscar was overjoyed! The village shared in his happiness. Everyone would get money for supplies. The school would be rebuilt. School books would be replaced.

Oscar's dream had come true!

# Comprehension Check

## Summarize

Reread "The Sheep Herder."
Summarize.

## Think About It

1. What did you think Oscar was going to do at different times?

| What I Predict | What Happens |
|---|---|
|  |  |
|  |  |
|  |  |

2. Why couldn't Oscar go to school after the mud slide?

3. If you lived in Oscar's village, how would you have helped?

## Write About It

Do you think it is important to help other people? Why?

# Skills and Strategies

## Decoding

Read the words.

| | | | |
|---|---|---|---|
| town | enjoy | loud | sound |
| ground | down | spout | brown |
| frown | found | crown | coin |

## Vocabulary

| | |
|---|---|
| bound | impossible |
| control | able |

## Comprehension

**Description** Authors give information to support a topic sentence. A Description Web helps you organize information.

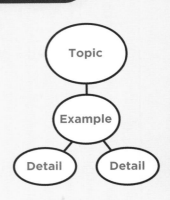

Describe Bud's house.

# Bud's House

Bud Beaver waddled along the bank of a stream. He was bound to run into the loudest part. Suddenly, he could hear it. It was impossible to ignore. He was not able to control himself. It was time to build a new house!

He cut and dragged branches to the stream. He pounded down mud with his tail. Finally, his house was complete.

Fill in the **Description Web** for "Bud's House." Summarize.

# Busy Beavers

**by Donna Taglieri**
**illustrated by Diane Blasius**

## Building Dams

Beavers build dams like people build houses. They live by streams in woody places.

Beavers cut down branches with their teeth. Then they drag the branches out and make a dam. Why do they do this? Beavers try to stop the loud noise of rushing water by making a dam. It is an instinct.

When beavers are on land, they don't move quickly. Their thick tails are stiff and can get in the way. Beavers do not spend much time on the ground. They spend time swimming around.

Beavers have webbed feet and long flat tails. The flat tails help them swim fast. The tails also make beavers able to stand on their hind legs. Beavers pound their tails on the water when they are frightened. You can hear that loud sound from far away.

Beavers have long, sharp teeth. Their teeth help them cut branches from trees and bushes.

Beavers are expert builders. They use twigs and branches they have found to make dams. They take those branches in the water and make a big pile. Then they use mud to pack the dam so water can't get in.

It might seem impossible, but these dams can be as high as ten feet! You may think that beavers use just logs and sticks to make dams. But they use other things as well.

Some of these things can be sharp. Beavers can get hurt by rusty nails. They can choke on plastic bags. This is why we must unite to keep streams and rivers clean.

## A Spring Pond

Beavers can control water and make a pond. They do this by building a dam.

To make the dam, the beavers gather branches. Then they pack them with mud, moist soil, and leaves. This holds back the water.

When the water stops, it pools and makes a deep pond.

The new pond can be home for wetland animals. Fish, ducks, and frogs use the pond. Frogs lay eggs, and birds make nests there. A thirsty moose might stop by and take a drink.

Beaver dams help plants as well. When the stream is dammed, plants bloom on the muddy shores.

When summer ends, beavers make houses under and above water. These houses are called lodges.

A lodge is shaped like a rounded tent. It is made of sticks, twigs, and mud. A lodge can be placed on a lake shore or near a dam. Beavers use lodges to store food. A lodge is bound to be a safe place.

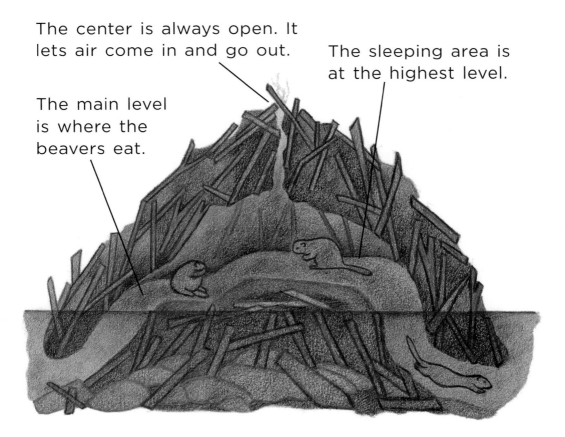

The center is always open. It lets air come in and go out.

The sleeping area is at the highest level.

The main level is where the beavers eat.

When you are in the woods, you
might spot a beaver's dam. If you see
one, a beaver may be close by.

Beavers can be shy. But you just
might get lucky and see one.

# Comprehension Check

## Summarize

Reread "Busy Beavers" again. Make a topic sentence about beavers. Use the Description Web to show details and examples.

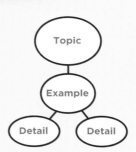

## Think About It

1. How are dams good for animals?

2. Why do beavers make dams?

3. What sort of home would you make for yourself? Explain.

## Write About It

How can a dam change a river?

# Skills and Strategies

## Decoding

Read the words.

| | | | |
|---|---|---|---|
| fault | small | sauce | crawl |
| jigsaw | install | straw | faucet |
| hallway | dawn | cause | walnut |

## Vocabulary

| | | |
|---|---|---|
| change | thoughtful | laundry |
| system | keep track | recalled |

## Comprehension

**Analyze Theme** Writers put messages in their writing. Those messages are called themes. A Theme Map helps you find clues to the theme.

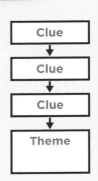

Look for the story's theme.

## A Present for Mom

"I don't have any money to get Mom a present," said Jamal. "I don't even have any change."

His sister Rose looked thoughtful. "Well, Mom likes a clean living room," she recalled. "Let's make a system."

Rose began to fold laundry. "You sweep. Keep track of time!"

Mom came in. She cried, "This is the best present I've ever gotten!"

Fill in a **Theme Map** for "A Present for Mom." Summarize.

# Talking to Mrs. Dawson

**by Carrie Dillon**
**illustrated by Kevin McGovern**

## Helping Out

Walt and Wendy lived with their mom in a big city. They lived in a tall building.

Mrs. Dawson lived upstairs. One day she saw them in the hallway. She called out to them.

"My knees hurt a lot today. It is impossible for me to get to the store. Would you go and pick up a few things for me?

"Yes," said Wendy. "We were just going to the store with Mom."

Mrs. Dawson handed Walt a list and money.

"We will be back soon," said Walt.

Mom was waiting for them. Walt and Wendy told her about Mrs. Dawson.

"She is a nice lady," added Mom. "When I was small, she would make rice and beans for us. It was hard for my mom to cook after a long day. My mom always thanked her for her kind deeds."

"We can do a kind deed for her!" exclaimed Walt.

Shopping for Mrs. Dawson was fun!

Mom paid for the food on her own list.

Walt paid for Mrs. Dawson's food with money she had given him. He got a few coins back as change.

Walt and Wendy carried bags up to Mrs. Dawson's place.

"Thank you," she said. "You may keep the change."

"We wanted to help. We didn't expect to get paid," explained Wendy.

"That's very thoughtful," said Mrs. Dawson. "You have been very kind. I know a lot more folks who can use your help."

## Helping Others

Soon Walt and Wendy were helping many people. Mr. Boil was not able to go shopping. Miss Miller asked them to take her laundry to the dry cleaners.

Miss Sharp had a bad sore throat. She talked uneasily in a low voice. She asked Wendy to call someone to fix a leaky pipe.

Wendy and Walt were busy and proud. They were helping people who needed help.

They set up a system for running to the store. Walt would keep track of the shopping lists. Wendy kept track of the money.

One night, Walt and Wendy were resting after working all day. The phone rang and Mom picked it up.

"Mrs. Dawson asked us to go upstairs. It sounds important," said Mom.

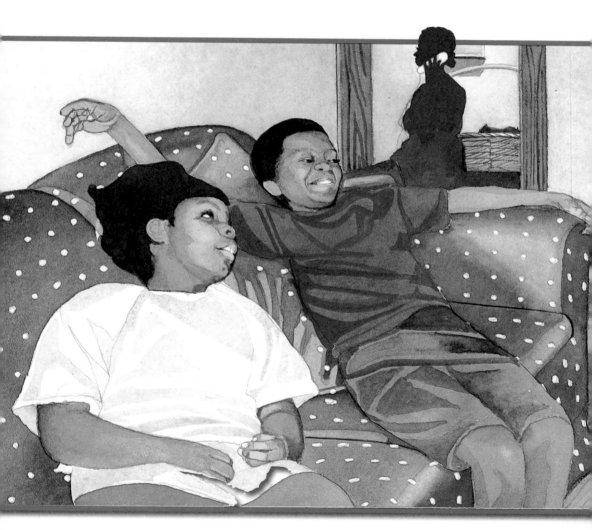

All the people Walt and Wendy had helped were with Mrs. Dawson. Cake, ice cream, and punch were on the table. Everyone helped themselves.

"This is just like when I was small," recalled Mom. "But this time Mrs. Dawson's treats are for my thoughtful kids!"

# Comprehension Check

## Summarize

Reread "Talking to Mrs. Dawson." Fill in character, setting, and plot in the Theme Map. Summarize.

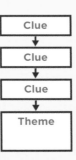

| Clue |
|------|
| Clue |
| Clue |
| Theme |

## Think About It

1. How were Wendy and Walt helpful?

2. Why did so many people in their building need help?

3. How does it make you feel to help people? Why?

## Write About It

How could you help out older people in your community? Explain.

# Skills and Strategies

## Decoding

Read the words.

| | | | |
|---|---|---|---|
| scratch | splash | splinter | throat |
| chimp | scrub | thrill | sprinkle |
| graph | spread | sprain | three |

## Vocabulary

| | | |
|---|---|---|
| couple | certain | attention |
| prowled | bothering | yesterday |

## Comprehension

**Make Judgments**

| Action | → | Judgment |
|---|---|---|
| | → | |

Sometimes writers don't say what they think of a character. It is up to you to form an opinion of the characters. A Judgment Chart helps you judge a character's actions.

What judgments are made about Dan?

# Sleeping Duck

Pam Peacock called, "Dan! Look! I had my feathers done yesterday!" Dan Duck watched a couple of clouds.

Sid Skunk prowled past. "Pay attention. I'm certain Pam was talking to you." But Dan just stretched. Sid and Pam left.

Dan woke up. "Oh no," he cried. "I must have slept with my eyes open again!"

Fill out a **Judgment Chart** for "Sleeping Duck." Summarize.

# Howie Helps Out

**by David Brent**

**illustrated by James Williamson**

## A Party for Gus

It was a proud day. The animals were throwing a party for Gus the lizard. Gus was famous for his thoughtful deeds.

Everyone was glad, except a couple of chimps. They were unhappy. They wore big frowns on their faces. Why did Gus get all the attention?

The unhappiest chimp was named Howie. He liked to clown around and tease other animals. Howie did not know Gus, but he was certain he wouldn't like Gus.

"That Gus is too nice. I wish I could make everyone dislike him. I know! I will say he stole my lunch. Then the animals are bound to distrust him."

Howie went to talk with Flump, the Toad. "With that mouth, he can tell everyone what a bad pal Gus is," thought Howie.

"Hi Flump," Howie shouted. "Gus stole my lunch yesterday."

"Don't be silly," replied Flump. "I had lunch with Gus right here. We ate flies on this rock. Now leave."

Howie went to Jack the Jackal as he prowled about.

"Stop bothering me. I can't prowl with you bouncing around me," growled Jack.

"I'm trying to tell you that Gus is a bad lizard. He makes all the ducks cry."

The lion cubs were listening. "That's not right! We saw Gus playing with the ducks three days ago."

Howie slunk off.

Howie tried to make the bulls think
that Gus had taken all their yams. He
put the yams in a basket high on a hill.
Then he ran down to the bulls.

"I saw Gus take all your yams!"
Howie called out.

"We just saw you put them in a
basket up there! We're going to tell the
king," they cried.

## Howie Meets Gus

Everyone gathered to discuss Howie's tales. King Stripes sat on his throne.

"Why are you trying to hurt Gus?" he asked Howie.

"I just can't see why everybody likes him so much," Howie shrugged.

"Why don't you meet him? Maybe you will find out."

"All right," sighed Howie.

"Hey Gus!" Howie shouted as he swung on a vine. "Can we talk?"

"Let me help these ants get up the tree," said Gus.

"Why does he help everyone?" Howie asked Holly the Hippo.

"Just ask him," said Holly as she sank into the pond.

Gus screamed. Then, something amazing happened.

"I was helping the ants, and I slipped. I started to fall into the water," recalled Gus. "Howie swung in and saved me just in time!"

"I don't believe it," said Jerry the Giraffe.

"It's true," said Howie. "I found out that I like to help, too."

It was a very happy day. The animals planned a party to thank Howie for saving Gus's life.

# Comprehension Check

## Summarize

Reread "Howie Helps Out." Use the Judgment Chart. Summarize.

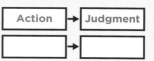

## Think About It

1. What did you first think about Howie?

2. Why didn't Howie's friends trust him?

3. How do people feel when they are tricked?

### ✏ Write About It

Tell about a time when you made a judgment about someone.

# Skills and Strategies

## Decoding

Read the words.

| | | | |
|---|---|---|---|
| brave | spray | right | late |
| arrive | train | milder | daylight |
| frighten | spy | plain | surprise |

## Vocabulary

| | | |
|---|---|---|
| Africa | boarded | languages |
| exercise | science | astronaut |

## Comprehension

**Problem and Solution** A problem is something that needs to be worked out. A solution fixes the problem. A Problem and Solution Chart helps you find the problems in a selection.

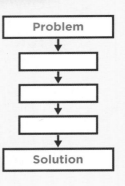

Find the problems and the solution.

# Making a Choice

"Which classes will you choose? I might take a class on Africa or maybe study French," said Kyle. He and Faith boarded the bus.

"I'm not good at languages. I like to exercise. But I should take an extra science class since I want to be an astronaut," said Faith.

"Okay. So you take science and I'll take French!" exclaimed Kyle.

Fill in a **Problem and Solution Chart** for "Making a Choice." Summarize.

# Mae on Board

## by Cassidy Blackfoot

Mae Jemison had a big problem. She was afraid of high places. But she had to take an elevated train to her dance classes. She climbed up and up and up, and soon she was on the train.

Mae's love of dance helped her be brave. She didn't know then that being brave would help her go to space.

## A Dream of Space

Mae always wanted to go to space. When she was five years old, she told her teacher she wanted to be a scientist.

This wish got her teacher's attention. In 1961, many girls had fewer choices than they have now. Few found jobs in science. And she did not know of any female astronauts. But Mae was certain of her goal.

Mae studied science in college. She also studied languages and African history.

Mae decided to become a doctor. After she got her degree, she joined the Peace Corps. With the Peace Corps, she treated sick people in Africa. She helped them stay well.

| Mae Jemison Time Line | |
|---|---|
| 1956 | Mae is born on October 17 in Alabama. |
| 1959 | Her family moves to Chicago. |
| 1973 | She goes to Stanford University on scholarship. |
| 1982 | She graduates from college and enters the Peace Corps. |
| 1987 | Mae enters NASA's astronaut training program. |
| 1992 | She flies into space on September 12 aboard the Endeavour. |

Mae prepares to climb out of her T-38 training jet.

Mae went back to school when she returned to the US. She still wanted to visit space. She tried to get into the space program, but she was not chosen. Mae still felt strongly about it. She tried again and was accepted.

In 1987 Mae began training to fly in a space shuttle. She finished in 1988. In 1992 she climbed on board a space shuttle.

The space shuttle lifts off its launch pad at Kennedy Space Center.

## Part of Space and the Stars

Mae and six others boarded the space shuttle. It took off, and soon they were in space.

The shuttle went far from Earth into space. As it climbed, the stars grew brighter and brighter.

Mae looked back at Earth. She saw the sea. She thought, "I belong up here." She felt like part of space and the stars.

Mae had to get used to being on the shuttle. It is strange to float in the air. Mae's body would have weak muscles if she did not exercise.

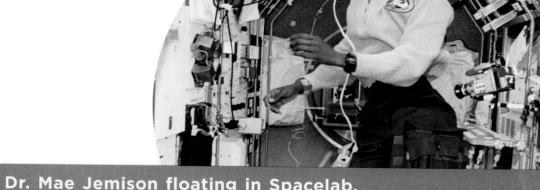

Dr. Mae Jemison floating in Spacelab.

Some astronauts ran or biked in place. Mae liked to jump and dance. When she jumped up, she didn't land right away. She spun around ten times because she was so light!

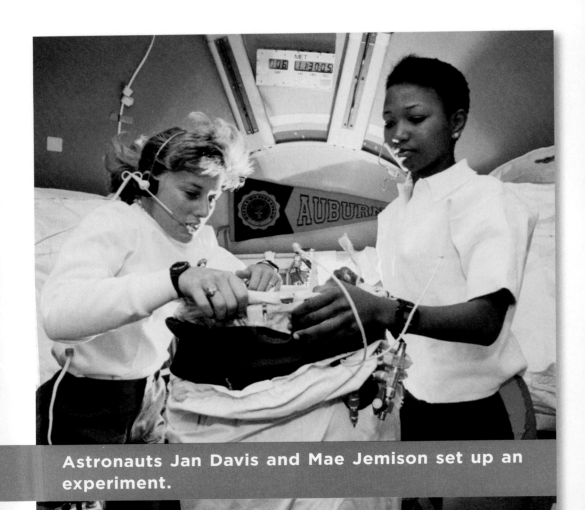
Astronauts Jan Davis and Mae Jemison set up an experiment.

But Mae had work to do on the shuttle. Her job was to run tests on bone cells. She had frogs and frog eggs on board. She watched to see if space changed how they grew. Her study would help others find ways to help sick people.

The Endeavor landed at Kennedy Space Center on September 20, 1992.

After a week, the shuttle returned. Mae was now the first African-American woman astronaut. She was very proud.

These days Dr. Mae Jemison teaches at universities. She also runs a science camp for children. She looks for ways to make life better for everyone.

Dr. Jemison found a way to visit space. Where will she go next?

# Comprehension Check

## Summarize

Reread "Mae on Board."
Fill in the Problem
and Solution Chart.
Summarize.

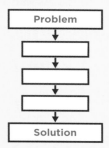

## Think About It

1. What happens in space if you don't exercise your muscles?

2. Why did girls have fewer job choices in 1961?

3. Which job of Mae's was the most interesting? Explain.

## Write About It

How did Mae help people?

# Skills and Strategies

## Decoding

Read the words.

| | | | |
|---|---|---|---|
| knew | slow | dream | stone |
| broom | teach | grew | crow |
| speech | close | stoop | throw |

## Vocabulary

Read the words.

| | | |
|---|---|---|
| strange | purpose | emotions |
| information | notice | |

## Comprehension

**Author's Purpose** An author writes to give information, to entertain, or to persuade. An Author's Purpose Chart helps you decide why the author wrote the selection.

| Clues |
|---|
| |
| |
| |

↓

| Author's Purpose |
|---|
| |

What is the author's purpose?

# Chimps in the Wild

Chimpanzees talk with their bodies. The strange sounds they make have a purpose. They send information and show emotions. A cry warns of danger. A loud bark tells others about food.

Notice how a frightened chimp will show its teeth. Chimps ask for food by holding out their hand. Chimps holding hands are friends.

Fill in the **Author's Purpose Chart** for "Chimps in the Wild." Summarize.

# Jane Goodall

## by Rod Harrington

## A Little Toy Chimp

"Look, Jane," called Jane's father. He gave his baby girl a toy chimp for her second birthday.

Friends claimed that the chimp would make Jane have bad dreams. But Jane liked the toy.

No one could know then that soon Jane Goodall would change how everybody thought about chimps.

It took a long time for the chimps to trust Jane.

Jane Goodall was born in England in 1934. She grew up reading books about animals.

By age eleven she knew she wanted to go to Africa. Her mother told her to work hard and she would find a way.

She worked and saved her money. She went to Africa when she was 23 years old.

Mary and Louis Leaky study animal bones and teeth.

In Africa, Jane met Dr. Louis Leakey. He was a scientist who studied how people lived in the past. Dr. Leakey gave Jane a job. Jane worked with him for a while.

Dr. Leakey told Jane about chimps. He wanted to gather information about how they lived. Jane made a decision to study the chimps in the rain forest.

In 1960 Jane went to Africa. She brought her mother with her. She went to work watching the chimps.

At first Jane had to be careful. If she came too close, chimps would notice her. Seeing a strange person might scare them. Jane waited and watched from far away. Little by little, chimps paid less attention to her. Jane moved closer.

Jane waits and watches as the chimps go about their daily life.

## Learning in the Jungle

One day Jane saw a strange thing. Two chimps had picked twigs from a tree. They peeled leaves off the twigs and used those twigs to fish for bugs from a nest.

Jane saw that these chimps made tools. Before, everybody thought only humans made tools. Jane wrote about how smart chimps were.

Jane watched the chimps work and play together. At times, they sat beside each other. Then they brushed each other's hair. Other times she saw them throw food just like babies throw toys.

Sometimes a mother chimp came over, carrying a sleepy baby chimp on her back.

At the end of the day, a mother chimp will play with her babies.

A mother chimp cuddles her baby.

Jane saw different emotions from chimps. Some acted funny. Some acted shy. Chimps surprised her, too. Some began to battle. But others were sweet and peaceful.

Jane gave them all names. A baby chimp named Mel had no family. Spindle was a single male. He was not much older than Mel. But Spindle cared for Mel.

Dr. Leakey had asked Jane to spend ten years studying chimps. She studied in Africa much longer.

Today Jane writes and gives speeches. She tells about how people can help the chimps.

Chimps live in rain forests. Rain forests are being cut down. Protection of rain forests will save chimps.

Rain forests are home to many kinds of plants and wildlife.

It is important to Jane that we care for all life on Earth.

In 1977 Jane started a group. Its purpose is to keep studying and helping chimps in Africa. It also teaches about helping people, animals, and the places where they live.

It all began with a toy chimp and a little girl. Jane still has that toy chimp in her home.

# Comprehension Check

## Summarize

Reread "Jane Goodall." Fill in the Author's Purpose Chart. Summarize.

| Clues |
|-------|
|       |
|       |
|       |

↓

| Author's Purpose |
|------------------|

## Think About It

1. What does the author want you to know about Jane Goodall?

2. Why was Jane's toy chimp important to the selection?

3. How can you tell animals have feelings?

## Write About It

Why was Jane Goodall's work important?

# Skills and Strategies

## Decoding

Read the words.

| | | | |
|---|---|---|---|
| without | tooth | author | threw |
| shawl | screw | frown | unhooked |
| zoo | cloud | stall | clown |

## Vocabulary

| | | |
|---|---|---|
| simple | hatch | adults |
| shrink | surface | |

## Comprehension

**Draw Conclusions** Readers use clues and what they know to understand what they read. The Conclusion Map helps you find clues in the selection.

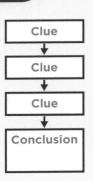

Clue
↓
Clue
↓
Clue
↓
Conclusion

Look for clues. Find a conclusion.

## Animal Mothers

Mothers teach their babies simple skills.

Sea turtle mothers lay round eggs beneath the surface of the sand. Then the new turtles hatch and crawl across the brown sand to the sea.

A frog doesn't always need its mother. It hatches from an egg as a tadpole. Its tail shrinks and it grows legs as it becomes an adult.

Fill in the **Conclusions Map** for "Animal Mothers." Summarize.

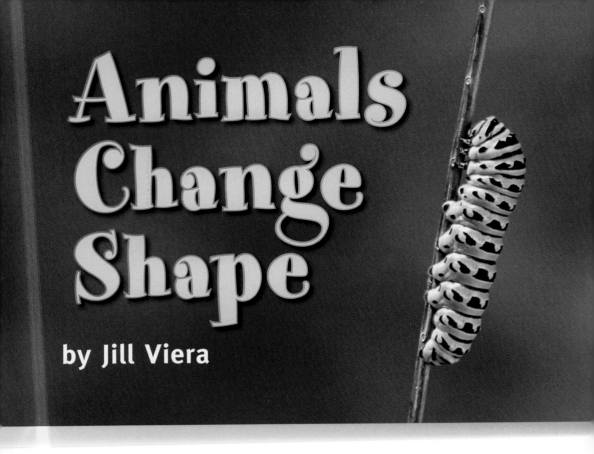

# Animals Change Shape

### by Jill Viera

## Life Cycles

A butterfly is a wonderful sight on a summer day. But did you know that it started as a simple caterpillar? The caterpillar came from an egg.

The shape of the body on some animals changes as it grows. Other animals, like dogs, keep the shapes they were born with. They just grow larger.

A caterpillar grows wings
and changes into a butterfly

All animals have life cycles. A life cycle is how an animal changes as it grows older.

A caterpillar hatches from an egg. Then it makes a hard case around itself. When it comes out of the hard case, it is a butterfly. Then the butterfly lays eggs and the cycle starts again.

Some grasshoppers shed their skins six times!

## Grasshoppers

A grasshopper also changes during its life cycle. Grasshoppers hatch from eggs. They look a little like grasshoppers, but they do not have wings. Only when they become adults do grasshoppers get their wings.

Each mother grasshopper can lay about 100 eggs!

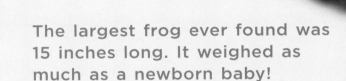

The largest frog ever found was 15 inches long. It weighed as much as a newborn baby!

## Tadpoles and Frogs

A frog's shape also changes after it is born. When a frog hatches from an egg, it is called a tadpole. It looks like a little fish without fins. It has a tail but it does not have legs. Soon it will grow legs.

Frogs need their long legs to hop away from snakes and large birds.

Once the tadpole has legs, it is called a froglet. A froglet still has a long tail. It might look strange with a tail and legs. Soon the tail will shrink into the body as the frog grows. Its legs will get bigger. Then it will look like a grown-up frog.

Some frogs can lay up to 30,000 eggs. Many eggs will be eaten by fish and other animals.

# Sea Turtles

Sea turtles come from eggs, too. A baby sea turtle uses an egg tooth to help it hatch. The egg tooth looks like a horn on its face. The baby turtle loses this tooth soon after birth.

Green sea turtles lay their eggs on the beach where they were born. They lay from 80 to 120 eggs.

It can take three to seven days for a baby turtle to dig out of the sand.

Jellyfish, shrimp, and fish might swim by and eat up the small blue crabs.

## Blue Crabs

A blue crab is born from an egg as well. It is called a larva. When it hatches it has no shell and tiny legs. The larva does not walk on the bottom of the ocean like a crab. Instead, it floats on the surface of the water.

It takes about a month for the larva to grow legs and start growing a shell.

The blue crab grows its eight legs and two claws. It looks more like a crab, but at first it has no color. It turns brown as its shell hardens and it gets bigger.

It eats clams, shrimp, and some plants. It will lay its eggs in a salty wetland.

An adult blue crab can regrow a leg it has lost.

Some animals have big changes in their shape as they get older. Some animals just lose a tooth or grow wings. Some animals just get larger. Which animal are you?

# Comprehension Check

## Summarize

Reread "Animals Change Shape." Fill in the Conclusions Chart. Summarize.

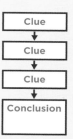

## Think About It

1. What conclusions about animals did the author draw?

2. Why do you think a frog lays so many eggs?

3. What other animals change shape during their lives?

## Write About It

How do people change as they get older?

# Skills and Strategies

| TITLE | DECODING | VOCABULARY | COMPREHENSION |
|---|---|---|---|
| **Unit 1    pages 6–61** | | | |
| 6    A Big Jam | /a/a p<u>a</u>ck, /i/i sp<u>i</u>ll | jam, tip, feel, ran into, quit, acting | Analyze Story Structure: Character, Setting, Plot |
| 16    Pen Pals | /e/e g<u>e</u>t, /o/o p<u>o</u>t, /u/u c<u>u</u>t | letters, visit, treks, plans, explorer | Analyze Story Structure: Character, Setting, Plot |
| 26    Ant Tricks | Beginning blends | slim, objects, smart, pests | Summarize: Main Idea and Details |
| 38    Wetlands | /ā/a_e s<u>a</u>m<u>e</u> | wetlands, bills, tide, lungs | Summarize: Main Idea and Details |
| 50    Jake's Pets | /ī/i_e l<u>i</u>k<u>e</u> | decide, trap, hissed, gazed | Analyze Story Structure: Problem and Solution |
| **Unit 2    pages 62–121** | | | |
| 62    Miss Pope's Class Puts on a Play | /ō/o_e st<u>o</u>v<u>e</u>, /ū/u_e t<u>u</u>n<u>e</u> | practice, crowd, skilled, close, set, roles | Generate Questions: Summarize |
| 74    Mom Wolf Speaks | /ē/e sh<u>e</u>, ea dr<u>ea</u>m, ee s<u>ee</u>m, y happ<u>y</u> | deeds, trust, usually, gleamed, sunset | Generate Questions: Fantasy and Reality |
| 86    Flight: Gliders to Jets | /ī/i qu<u>i</u>et, igh s<u>igh</u>t, y tr<u>y</u> | early, different, hobbies, sights, plastic, blades | Summarize: Fact and Opinion |
| 98    Animal Hide and Seek | CCVCC | danger, clump, cling, swift, scales | Generate Questions: Summarize |
| 110    Ben Franklin | /ā/ai m<u>ai</u>n, ay st<u>ay</u> | draft, invented, flames, routes, habits | Summarize: Author's Purpose |
| **Unit 3    pages 122–181** | | | |
| 122    A Slow Feast | Long /ō/o t<u>o</u>ld, oa b<u>oa</u>t, ow <u>ow</u>n | midday, large, complete, feast | Visualize: Make Inferences |
| 134    Chet Mantis's Hunt | /ch/ch whi<u>ch</u>, tch pa<u>tch</u> | coast is clear, office, clutched, boasted, unlatched | Analyze Story Structure: Plot and Setting |
| 146    The Everglades | /th/th wi<u>th</u>; /hw/wh <u>wh</u>en | river, protect, beneath, drained, pounds, wildlife | Analyze Text Structure: Cause and Effect |
| 158    Brent's Pictures | /s/c spa<u>c</u>e, /j/g ju<u>dg</u>e | ancient, mist, imagined, ledge, amazing, tilted | Visualize: Make Inferences |
| 170    Trish's Triumph | /f/ph <u>ph</u>one, /sh/sh bru<u>sh</u> | ramp, perfect, sketches, gathered, idea, triumph | Analyze Text Structure: Sequence |

| TITLE | DECODING | VOCABULARY | COMPREHENSION |
|-------|----------|------------|---------------|
| **Unit 4    pages 182–241** | | | |
| 182  A Splendid Meal | /skr/*scr* <u>scr</u>eam, /spl/*spl* <u>spl</u>ash, /spr/*spr* <u>spr</u>ing, /str/*str* <u>str</u>etch | recipe, rise, splendid, flat as a pancake, batter | Make Inferences and Analyze: Compare and Contrast |
| 194  Weaver's Lessons | /n/*kn* <u>kn</u>ow, /r/*wr* <u>wr</u>ite | get along, wring, wrap, earn, beamed, passed | Make Inferences and Analyze: Draw Conclusions |
| 206  Be Smart: Save Water! | /är/*ar* st<u>ar</u>t | supply, dusk, tap, liquids, remember, stream | Monitor Comprehension: Compare & Contrast |
| 218  Helping Out | /ôr/*or* f<u>or</u>, *ore* st<u>ore</u> | ignored, chore, talents, collected, projects, agree | Monitor Comprehension: Author's Purpose |
| 230  The Perfect Hideaway | /ûr/*er* inf<u>er</u>, *ir* f<u>ir</u>st, *ur* s<u>ur</u>f | bored, wonder, perked, shady | Monitor Comprehension: Make and Confirm Predictions |
| **Unit 5    pages 242–301** | | | |
| 242  The Great Ice Cream Shop Turn Around | /ā/*a*, /ē/*e*, /ī/*i*, /ō/*o*, and /ū/*u* Open syllables | special, owned, nearby, customers, demanded, survive | Summarize: Sequence |
| 254  Dolores Huerta: She Took a Stand | /u̇/*oo* b<u>oo</u>k | childhood, united, laws, important, basic | Make Inferences and Analyze: Cause & Effect |
| 266  Hot–Air Balloons | /ü/*ew* cr<u>ew</u>, *oo* b<u>oo</u>t | crew, designs, interest, pilot, breathe | Make Inferences and Analyze: Fact and Opinion |
| 278  The Sheep Herder | /oi/*oi* s<u>oi</u>l, *oy* b<u>oy</u> | village, expert, guided, distant, soil, listened | Make Inferences and Analyze: Make and Confirm Predictions |
| 290  Busy Beavers | /ou/*ou* r<u>ou</u>nd, *ow* br<u>ow</u>n | bound, control, able, impossible | Summarize: Description |
| **Unit 6    pages 302–361** | | | |
| 302  Talking to Mrs. Dawson | /ô/*au* p<u>au</u>se, *aw* cl<u>aw</u>, /ôl/*al* s<u>al</u>t | change, keep, track, recalled, system, laundry, thoughtful | Analyze Story Structure: Theme |
| 314  Howie Helps Out | Review: blends and digraphs | couple, attention, certain, yesterday, prowled, bothering | Monitor Comprehension: Make Judgments |
| 326  Mae on Board | Review: /ā/, /ī/ | Africa, science, languages, boarded, astronaut, exercise | Analyze Text Structure: Problem and Solution |
| 338  Jane Goodall | Review:  /ē/, /ō/, /ū/ | strange, purpose, emotions, notice, information | Monitor Comprehension: Author's Purpose |
| 350  Animals Change Shape | Review: variant vowels | simple, hatch, adults, shrink, surface | Monitor Comprehension: Draw Conclusions |

# ACKNOWLEDGMENTS

**ILLUSTRATIONS**

7-14: Heather Maione. 17-24: Julie Ecklund. 51-60: Susan Hartung. 63-72: Priscilla Burris. 75-84: Marianne M. Sachs-Iacob. 87-96: Dick Smolinski. 99-108: Karen Bell. 111-120: Susan Avishai. 123-132: Robert Neubacker. 135-144: Marc Mongeau. 147-156: Robert Casilla. 159-168: Will Sweeney. 171-180: Lorraine Sylvestri. 183-192: Dom & Keunhee Lee. 195-204: Arvis Stewart. 219-228: Sally Springer. 231-240: Daniel Vasconcelleos. 243-252: Deborah Melmon. 255-264: Robert Casilla. 279-288: Robert Casilla. 291-300 Diane Blasius. 303-312: Kevin McGovern. 315-324: James Williamson.

---

**PHOTOGRAPHY**

*All photographs are by Macmillan/McGraw Hill (MMH) except as noted below:*

3: (t) age fotostock/SuperStock; (b) Michael Sewell/Peter Arnold, Inc.; 4: (tl) StockTrek/Getty Images; (bl) Danita Delimont/Alamy; 5: (tr) PhotoLink/Getty Images; (br) Roger Ressmeyer/CORBIS; 27: Peter Arnold, Inc./Alamy; 28: © age fotostock/SuperStock; 29: Bob Anderson/Masterfile; 30: Peter Arnold, Inc./Alamy; 31: © age fotostock/SuperStock; 32: kris Mercer/Alamy; 33: Susan E. Degginger/Alamy; 34: (t) Karen Tweedy-Holmes/CORBIS;  (b) Anthony Bannister/Gallo Images/CORBIS; 35: Karen Tweedy-Holmes/CORBIS; 36: (t) eStock Photo/PictureQuest; (b) Andrew Mounter/Getty Images; 39: Joe McDonald/CORBIS; 40: Index Stock Imagery/PictureQuest; 41: Valerie Giles/Photo Researchers, Inc.; 42: Joe McDonald/CORBIS; 43: Joe McDonald/Bruce Coleman, Inc.; 44: Tim Zurowski/CORBIS; 45: (t) Royalty-Free/CORBIS; (inset) Andrew J. Martinez/Photo Researchers, Inc.; 46: Age Fotostock/Super Stock; 47: Joe McDonald/CORBIS; 48: Michael Sewell/Peter Arnold, Inc.; 87: Royalty-Free/CORBIS; 88: (bkgd) PhotoLink/Getty Images; 90: (t) Royalty-Free/CORBIS; (bkgd) PhotoLink/Getty Images; 91: (t) Paul Dopson/AirTeamImages; (bkgd) PhotoLink/Getty Images; 92: (t) Design Pics Inc./Alamy; (bkgd) PhotoLink/Getty Images; 93: (t) Museum of Flight/CORBIS; (bkgd) PhotoLink/Getty Images; 94: (t) © imageshop - zefa visual media uk ltd/Alamy; (bkgd) PhotoLink/Getty Images; 95: (t) Antony Nettle/Alamy; (bkgd) PhotoLink/Getty Images; 96: (t) NASA/Getty Images; (bkgd) PhotoLink/Getty Images; 114: Chuck Pefley/Alamy; 115: Royalty-Free/CORBIS; 118: Wesley Hitt/Alamy; 119: MPI/Getty Images; 207: StockTrek/Getty Images; 209: © Mike Brinson/Getty Images; 211: © Tom Stewart/CORBIS; 212: Danita Delimont/Alamy; 213: (b) John Downer/Getty Images; (inset) Paul & Joyce Berquist/Animals Animals; 214: David Muench/CORBIS; 216: © StockTrek/Getty Images; 267: Chris McLennan/Alamy; 268: Dennis Frates/Alamy; 269: Sheila Terry/Photo Researchers Inc.; 270: CORBIS; 271: imagestate/Alamy; 272: Holt Studios International Ltd/Alamy; 273: Travel Ink/Alamy; 274: Randy Wells/Getty Images; 275: DEPL Images/Alamy; 276: Chris McLennan/Alamy; 315: Photodisc/Getty Images; 327: © CORBIS; 328-329: © Masterfile (Royalty-Free Div.); 329: Bettmann/CORBIS; 331: ROBERT SULLIVAN/AFP/Getty Images; 332: Roger Ressmeyer/CORBIS; 333: NASA/Roger Ressmeyer/CORBIS; 334: NASA/Roger Ressmeyer/CORBIS; 335: CORBIS; 336: China Photos/Getty Images; 339: Martin Harvey/Gallo Images/CORBIS; 340: Martin Harvey/Alamy; 341: Bettmann/CORBIS; 342: Bettmann/CORBIS; 343: Karl Ammann/CORBIS; 344: BRUCE COLEMAN INC./Alamy; 345: Danita Delimont/Alamy; 346: Martin Harvey/Gallo Images/CORBIS; 347: PETER PAYNE/UNEP/Peter Arnold, Inc.; 348: BIOS/Peter Arnold, Inc.; 351: KEVIN AITKEN/Peter Arnold, Inc.; 352-353: Ralph A. Clevenger/CORBIS; 354: (tl) George D. Lepp/CORBIS; 354-355: Jim Zipp/Photo Researchers, Inc.; 356: Hans Pfletschinger/Peter Arnold, Inc.; 357: KEVIN AITKEN/Peter Arnold, Inc.; 358: Lynda Richardson/CORBIS; 359: Millard H. Sharp/Photo Researchers, Inc.; 360: Bredt Covitz.